Paws
for
Thought

Jane Wheeler

ISBN 978-1-955156-14-1 (paperback)
ISBN 978-1-955156-15-8 (hardcover)
ISBN 978-1-955156-16-5 (digital)

Rushmore Press LLC
1 800 460 9188
www.rushmorepress.com

Printed in the United States of America

To Sam and Carolyn

This is a book about a dog, on the one hand, and about me and my life on the other, but mostly about the lessons I have learned over the years I've spent with my dog, and without her.

In her own unassuming way, Zoey has been a guide dog – not in the usual ways that spring to mind, wherein we envision a placid and meticulously mannered seeing-eye dog escorting a blind person across a busy intersection, or a Lassie, fully attuned to the needs of her masters, fetching help from a neighboring farm when her family is in trouble – but in a subtler, and probably more common, way that dogs have of nudging us to our inner guidance.

We all have a guidance system, either buried deep within us or clearly visible, that steers us along the sometimes straight, sometimes zigzag, course of our personal journeys. Some of us go to church regularly, follow religious practices, or take care to adhere to certain ethical principles. This is one version of guidance, an external form that brings considerable security. Many of us, however, navigate through our lives without the clarity that such constructs provide. We may have strong values and beliefs, but our guiding sonars refuse to send us a straightforward roadmap. We flip flop, we waffle, we scan the horizon for landmarks, and scope our surroundings for guideposts.

Enter, the dog. Studies have shown that dogs are good for our physical health: owning a dog is associated with lower blood pressure, lower triglyceride and cholesterol levels, better mental health, and even specific benefits like improved rates of survival following cardiac arrest. Dog therapy has been studied for its value in care of the elderly, and enlightened nursing homes now include this health care "modality" in the spectrum of services they offer. At the other end of the lifespan, dogs are again called into service; in hospitals and other clinical settings, children's wards use dog therapy to brighten spirits and quicken recovery. Our society acknowledges – for the very young and the very old – the natural guidance of dogs, their beneficial impact on mental and physical health.

Scientific research has yet to prove that dogs have an equally, and possibly more, profound impact on our spiritual health. They model for us some of the most important characteristics that we aspire to, though we express them as human, rather than canine, beings. Unconditional love, trust, support, steadfastness, loyalty, even joie de vivre – these come effortlessly to our furry companions.

By contrast, it takes some of us years to learn these fundamental life lessons, and to embody, however imperfectly, the characteristics and the simple way of being that radiate so naturally in and through a dog. I, for one, have decades of effort behind me. My dog, in her short nine years, has not only outpaced me but she has illuminated where my next steps lie. In the pages ahead, I hope to record some of the wisdom she has imparted.

1

I once had a dog, Zoey. Actually, she's relaxing not far from me now, curled up in a patch of sunshine on our light tan, wall-to-wall carpeting, worn and faded by over a decade under the feet of young children, a constant parade of their friends, neighbor dogs and their respective owners. For the past hour, she had been nestled in her oval doggie bed, her paws tucked under her muzzle and tail neatly wrapped under her belly, a picture of contentment. And then, a few moments ago, she relocated to this spot near me, to bask in the sun's warmth on this chilly January morning. Her presence is so tangible: her fur that stays sleek, mostly a bright white, despite the fact that her last bath was months ago, whimsically splotched with a few black patches; her body, devoid of all exertion; her rib cage, well articulated on her slim frame, which gently rises and falls in step with her breathing; her shiny wet black nose, adding an inescapable cuteness. She sighs in pleasure as she settles onto the floor, stretched out to absorb as many rays of thin winter sunshine as possible.

Why, then, do I say "once?" The nearness of death has a way of bringing a whole life, in its fullness, into panoramic view. Its sheer imminence leads us, whether in a state of sad reflection or active rejection, to connect the dots from past to future. As I gaze at nine-year-old Zoey today, I am joined by Zoey the eight-week-old puppy, adorable, a tiny package of playful, romping, baby animal nature; by Zoey as a young dog, patiently enduring the roughness of toddlers, saving her own play for a select few of her dog friends; by Zoey as a mature adult, accompanying me on my infinite missions on foot and in car. Even the grimness of her prognosis can't prevent inner smiles from bubbling up from the depths of my heart, as I remember Zoey in her many stages. The various manifestations of her being overlap like a collage of images, like phases of the moon, like a kaleidoscope, but reality, like a wave on the sand, sweeps the images away just as I appreciate, and want to hold onto, their beauty.

As a primary companion in the high noon of my life, Zoey has risen to meet the challenges of my emotional needs through thick and thin, with resolute patience, gracefully performing this service in the guise of *me* taking care of *her*. Dogs, it seems, permit their humans this absurd notion, this inversion of roles, and they do so with wordless humility.

The Dog Walk is a prime example. In this ritual well-known to nearly every dog owner, we believe ourselves to be "responsible" for our dogs. We arrange our lives around this simple mundane event, embed it into our daily schedules, mark out the passing of time not with coffee spoons, as T.S. Elliott would have it, but with dog walks. Dogs provide us with this organizing principle without discrimination or judgment – they never ask if we are *good* at walking – they simply present us with a basic factual need. (It is, after all, *the dog* who needs to go out, whose "business" must be accomplished.) Who benefits most from the arrangement is far from clear. We humans believe we know; it is *we*, after all, who walk the dog, and not the other way around. I, for one, took this duty thoroughly to heart. Rain or shine, in the scorching heat of summer in the South, or in the raw pre-dawn darkness and chill of mid-winter mornings, Zoey would allow me, presumably, to walk her.

The details of life, for each of us, move in to embellish common patterns, patterns which we share with humanity (or with a subset of the human family) and which are at first, by their very nature, simple. The details, then, add color, depth, and texture to the pattern, differentiating us and our lives from those of our friends, family members, neighbors, and others known and unknown. The Dog Walk is no exception.

While my two children were in elementary school, Zoey and our neighbor dog, Polo, accompanied me, day in and day out, on a critical voyage – the fetching of the kids. We walked through our middle-class, small-town, neighborhood, up a gradual but steady hill, across lazy intersections breaking the sidewalk every six or seven houses, along a small footpath connecting road and playground. Our pace was determined, in large extent, by the urgent need (mine) to reach the schoolyard by 2:25 p.m. when, on the dot, a classic school bell released five hundred exuberant children. Our neighborhood contributed six or eight kids to the school population every year, and it was these who scanned the large paved area for a small white-and-black dog and a large mottled brown-and-black one. And me, admittedly of lesser importance.

On our mile-long voyage back to Oxford Hills, as some builder pretentiously dubbed our development, we formed a motley parade of several children, varying in size, two dogs (humorously mismatched), and one adult sporting several backpacks stuffed with books, papers, projects, clothing shed over the course of the day, remnants of lunches stuffed in crumpled paper bags. The homebound walk often took twice as long as the outbound one, despite being gradually downhill all the way. For while Zoey, Polo, and I made record time on the uphill voyage, determined to never arrive even a moment after the bell rang, on the return trip no such pressures remained; the day was, essentially, over.

This daily journey, a mission of three, apparently did not go unappreciated. Once, in the grocery store, a woman stopped her cart mid-aisle to pass along to me her preschooler's observation, "Mommy, look at those dogs walking that lady." Was he right?

Symbiosis might better describe the relationship between dogs and humans than does our usual anthropocentric view, in which the human, as owner, takes care of the dog, as pet. Perhaps, instead, we owe our dogs gratitude for accepting us as we are, forgiving us our transgressions and shortcomings (if even noticing them), and permitting our petty arrogance. It takes, sometimes, an "other" to expose our growth edges to ourselves; dogs can also serve this positive, though uncomfortable, function.

The Dog Walk, in my books, was non-negotiable. My ostensible rationale was that dogs, like humans, need exercise and, even more to the point, they depend upon us for their opportunities to relieve bladder and bowel. This is, of course, wholly reasonable. But a slippery slope runs from rationale to rationalization.

I remember one day, mid-February, donning a down vest under a goretex rain jacket, opening an umbrella, and clipping Zoey onto her leash. Unquestioning, she plodded along behind me, two houses down, across the street and turning left into the next cul-de-sac, around to the back of the house, onto the deck. My already wet and chilly fingers jimmied the key in the lock, to open the door into the small kitchen where Polo awaited, wiggly and ready after five or six hours in a gray, hard plastic kennel. Due to the nasty weather, this day, I brought Zoey in with me rather than clipping her leash to a deck chair – a special treat. Polo, this day like every day, was delighted to see us. His collar slipped over his head and leash attached, we three headed out the door, into what was now freezing rain.

I should point out that neither Polo nor Zoey was, in my taxonomy of dogs, a hydrophilic dog. As I see it, there are dogs who love water (hydrophilic) and dogs who are fundamentally water-averse (hydrophobic), and there is no middle ground. About this, dogs are clear, totally lacking in ambivalence, and uninhibited in making their preferences known. Our walk was speedy. My jaw was set, my mind bound and determined to do this; the dogs dutiful, plodding, but uncomplaining. We arrived early, and took refuge under an overhang at the far edge of the school building, lower wing, next to the playground. Wind whipped around the edge of the building, turning my umbrella inside out. Freezing rain had now transitioned to large slushy snowflakes.

Standing pressed up against the brick side of the school, under these grim circumstances, my raw edges glared obvious. Had Zoey and Polo, these good souls, not been with me, I might have felt victorious in my ability to battle the elements, over-ride these weather-induced discomforts, and complete my mission. With them alongside me, I was forced to face the bleak hinterlands of my own compulsiveness. I apologized out loud to them both, explained my incapacities, asked them to forgive me, told them of my appreciation. Would this happen again? Probably. Over time, would kindness begin to win out over perceived need? Most certainly.

Zoey's cancer seemed to appear out of the clear blue, a hue which in retrospect looks naively lucid and somewhat darkened by denial. My past several months had been fraught with personal challenges that demanded my focus and depleted my energies. On top of the usual pressures confronting a single working mom, including the financial strain of music lessons, a calendar punctuated by birthday parties, children's feet that changed size every few months, and the ever-unfolding needs of a prematurely aging house, my 16-year-old son was deeply immersed in depression, and my boss, increasingly critical. Yes, the kids had pointed out "that ear thing" on Zoey. It might have been a month ago, or maybe even two or three. But my focus that fall had been fixed on the tasks before me: managing my children's ups and downs, keeping our home stable and hopefully peaceful, preparing an endless stream of family meals, commuting, writing grants and proposals on the job, washing and folding the laundry on the home front.

One morning, I noticed that the lump, now the size of an ordinary wild blueberry, perched on the very edge of Zoey's right ear, had bled overnight. The observation swooped in on me with a brutal intensity, as if a bucket of ice water had been thrown in my face (and remember, this was January). With my eyes now wide open and my perspective crystal clear, I snapped into action. At 9:00 a.m. sharp, I was on the phone scheduling an urgent visit with our vet. This led to an equally urgent follow-up visit to excise the lesion, reassurances from Dr. Kendall that the hated lump could well be benign, and discussions with two concerned kids about the post-operative care of a surgically wounded dog.

I should note that Zoey's ears are, hands down, one of her most adorable features. Perky triangular flaps, they stand upright at the base but then flop over upon themselves, folding at about the halfway point. They don't match; one is solid black, the other, white with black speckles. She communicates expressively with these ears, cocking them forward to show interest, lifting them when on alert, relaxing them against her head when at ease.

A first, chilling, blast of awareness arrived with the prospect of losing a portion of this beloved family member. Zoey without part of an ear? How would she look? Could we pat her just as well? Adore her as much? Be as proud of her? And how would she react?? Would she adapt and understand, in her own way, or would she grieve, failing to grasp that there is, in some sense she could never articulate, a reason for the change? The mother bear in me longed to protect my pup from physical mutilation. Life, even the life of an ear, always seeks to preserve itself – and our instincts tell us to honor this most basic of all desires. But my answer to Dr. Kendall was unequivocal: Yes, by all means we'll do whatever it takes to preserve her health. And herein came the sobering realization – my love for Zoey outweighed, in fact entirely eclipsed, her physical form.

Dr. Kendall's plan entailed putting Zoey under general anesthesia for the duration of what was innocuously called "the procedure." This never came to pass. On my way to work, I delivered our unsuspecting but highly suspicious pup into the hands of the kind-hearted, slightly nutty, Dr. Kendall, and sped the twelve miles between towns to my office and pile of work. Diligently revising a grant application, I attempted to tune out my concerns.

And then came the phone call. "Why didn't you tell me she had a lump on her shoulder, the size of a tennis ball?!," he accused. What? Now, I am quite familiar with tennis balls, having grown up in a New England family. No mere "game," tennis was a serious business, an athletic proving ground and the field of comparison between self and others; it required scrupulous form and continuous improvement. Tennis balls were a fixture in the house, an inescapable reality rather than a convenient image. Frankly, I had no idea what our vet was talking about. A lump the size of a tennis ball? And he's claiming that said lump is on her shoulder, not her ear. Later that day, perhaps to assuage my guilt for my own failure of attentiveness, I performed a quick reality check against the kids' observations. Did you notice a tennis ball-sized lump on Zoey? They looked at me blankly.

Warning signs that Zoey, like all living beings, floated in the stream of time, that she was not as I imagined her – a perennial puppy, exempt from the slow gentle force that relentlessly pulls Future into Present – had arisen before. Dogs, as they age, tend to grow warts in the same ways as humans, in their forties and beyond, grow skin tags. Neither are especially attractive, but we know them to be harmless. When we have them removed, it is usually for cosmetic reasons, to get rid of an unsightly reminder that we, too, at least in our physical form, are being morphed by time.

By this point, Zoey had had an unsightly wart, resembling an engorged tick, on her back for a couple of years. With Dr. Kendall's reassurance, I turned a blind eye. These things may happen, but no, they don't mean anything. I denied any underlying messages that Reality might be sending, messages about time, change, impermanence. This strategy worked just fine for several benign bumps hidden in random locations under Zoey's glossy fur. For the time being, ignorance had been bliss – though a bliss disquieted by a tinge of avoidance, a bliss more like intentional stability than unknowing carefreeness.

This time was different. They say that the universe delivers our lessons to us gently at first, that only if we refuse to learn from them in their mildest forms, do the lessons become increasingly clear, obvious, and even harsh. If we stand solid when brushed by a feather, we get whacked by a two-by-four and, if we are still standing strong after that, we get hit by an eighteen-wheeler. A friend of mine calls this the "having a piano drop on your head" experience. Is it cruel on the part of the universe, or is the universe just delivering to us the exact measure of guidance we have called for, the clarity we have shown we require, in order to learn? The escalation from nudge to jolt may be of our own making, the result of our decisions to ignore what is before us, to remain oblivious, to reject our lessons in their subtler, softer forms.

Zoey's tumor on her right shoulder arose over a matter of four or five days, between the initial visit with Dr. Kendall and her next appointment for the procedure. It had grown right before our eyes, yet somehow the three of us had failed to see it. Our vet, on the other hand, noticed this

Paws for Thought

game-changing development immediately. The scheduled surgery on Zoey's ear was called off. If the cancer has spread this quickly from ear to shoulder, he figured, what is the point of removing the tip of the iceberg?

A phone call later, I was back in the car, driving my commute in reverse order to pick up Zoey and bring her home, still intact but now, somehow, painfully vulnerable. Not one to sidestep the truth, Dr. Kendall blurted out a nightmare scenario: in his view, the most likely diagnosis for my beloved pup is an especially aggressive form of canine cancer, a mast cell tumor. These cancers move swiftly. If it has entered her bloodstream and traveled throughout her system, Zoey's cancer will continue to grow quickly and spread unpredictably, a ruthless invader, one virtually impossible to stop.

I have had to face grief before. A miscarriage after four months of pregnancy, just when I felt secure that I had made it into the clear, out of the risky first trimester and with a safe and still growing baby. The slow chilling death of my marriage, bringing down with it all of my heart's hopes and long-held visions, my picture of how my life would unfold. The ends of subsequent relationships on which, for a time anyway, I had built dreams of lasting love. How, then, am I caught so off guard?

2

In our house, shoes disappear on a regular basis. You might be tempted to blame this occurrence on the mayhem inherent in a house with two children, on the kids' tendency to unconsciously drop things wherever they are at the moment, or on a busy mom's haste and forgetfulness. But in reality, the culprit is Zoey.

To her defense, Zoey has never damaged a shoe, has never left so much as a tooth mark on a sneaker's rubber sole or a slight tear in its canvas upper. She seems to handle the contraband with care, almost respect. These items are, after all, relics of us, her Powers That Be. If not destruction, what is her crime? She cuddles.

Zoey is aware of being devious, and like any skillful criminal, she conceals her transgression. The shoe snatching happens only when we are out of the house, and fully out, not just in the back yard or upstairs sleeping. She does not want to be discovered in her naughtiness. To satisfy my curiosity, I once devised a plan to catch her in the act, red-pawed, as it were. Attempting to match her in cleverness, I exited through the garage door, as if to get in the car and drive away; instead, I walked a safe distance up the sidewalk and away from the house, made sure that I was out of view and, more importantly, out of sniffing range, waited a few minutes, then tiptoed back and opened the door silently. Quiet as a mouse, I somehow managed to escape her attention. Aha! I watched as, with a surreptitious air, Zoey padded into the laundry room where we (ostensibly) keep our shoes, made her selection from the numerous assorted choices, the majority of which were still in duplicate, gingerly picked one up with her teeth, and trotted, shoe in mouth, down the hall and across the living room to a favorite floor cushion. Arranging herself with typical precision, she settled comfortably into her characteristic curled-up pose. Curled up, now, around a well-worn sneaker, size six, several shades off white, with tie-dyed shoelaces.

The kids interpret Zoey's shoe choice as a badge of honor; he or she whose shoe has been taken is, for the moment, the Chosen One. Whoever finds that his or her shoe has been "disappeared," for doggie comfort or some obscure preference, flaunts the news as though it stands on a par with a major achievement or accolade, and visibly basks in the glow of this personal affirmation. Most of the time, though, the shoe Zoey absconds with is one of mine. I, too, melt a bit with the endearment implicit in this little foible. It is, after all, our dear doggie's particular eccentricity, something that is simply and totally "her," and

I – or, at least, something loosely related to me – have been involved.

It could be that I look fondly on Zoey's shoe obsession because, admittedly, I have my own eccentricities – a euphemism, perhaps, for my annoying and intractable habits. For one, I have a tendency to eat off my children's plates. Appalling, in my mother's eyes, worse even than slouching at the table or holding one's fork the wrong way. My children are alternately nonplused, peeved, triumphant at my lack of self control, and surprised at the existence of such blatant weakness in an adult. "Mom, you have *no will power*," my son has told me more than once, with smug satisfaction.

The roots of this foible run deep. In the family I grew up in, food substituted for nurturance. There was a good side to this, I suppose, which I mostly remember having to do with lots of homemade things – crunchy oatmeal raisin cookies; granola, dark brown because it was made with molasses rather than honey; and bread, always whole wheat and hearty, smelling comfortingly luscious as it baked. But food was also the battleground of control, wielded unilaterally by She who ruled the kitchen, my mother. The stakes of complying with, or reacting against, this control – namely, maternal favor – were high, and unquestioned. Add three girls, too close to each other in age, to this environment, and you have a recipe for, well, troubles.

Thus food in our family became the fall guy, the scapegoat on which much larger psychological issues got pinned; on the surface, these had to do with control – being controlled, that is, and utterly lacking it ourselves. At a deeper level, experienced as the murky waters of emotion but not yet understood in the daylight of the mind, they were about love and acceptance.

I remember one night when I was about six or seven years old; I was sitting at the dinner table, long after the others had left the dining room and the kitchen had been restored to order, facing a plate of homemade cranberry bread. I despised the stuff. Never mind that this was dessert; my mother had issued a dictum. Tears or no tears, I was not to leave the table until I had choked the thick slice down, every bite. Decades later, I still have a troubled relationship with cranberry bread, and more generally, the association between food and control (or lack thereof) remains, though in a much muted, and almost humorous, form: Don't tell me what to eat, and even more to the point, heaven forbid anyone tell me what *not* to eat. Am I proud of this? Hell, no. Do I try to overcome it? You bet. But as for progress, I give myself a B-. I am powerless before, say, the call of a chocolate chip cookie – and why stop at three?

Now Zoey, delightful, friendly, sweet Zoey, does have a tendency toward nervousness. Had she been a human child, we might have had her evaluated for an anxiety disorder, or considered whether or not she had a touch of OCD. We might have even solicited help for her in overcoming her dependency on shoes. Could she have managed her anxiety through appropriate medication, instead? Where does family support play into her recovery? Perhaps skillful therapy could have pinpointed the reasons for her urges, for her comfort-seeking behavior. Or maybe not. Then there's the perplexing thought that, if she could manage her emotional needs through drugs or talk therapy, Zoey might have actually moved beyond, maybe even completely dropped, her endearing habit of curling up with a shoe – and this, it turns out, feels not freeing and joyous, but sad.

All this tempers, a bit, my thinking about my own attachments. Who among us doesn't have an addiction, to some thing or another, to someone who might not even be good for us, to a way of thinking, a lifestyle, a behavior? I defy you to find one such unencumbered person, and then, go ahead and let him or her cast the first stone. I'd venture to say that, for most of us, our habitual patterns have become so integral to who we are that we are simply unaware of them. Our ways of talking, thinking, feeling, moving, and especially of judging, fearing, worrying, all take on a life of their own. They make their appearances, and exert their influence, of their own accord, as if we are on a sort of behavioral auto-pilot. Choice, in these cases, is a meaningless word – and change, well, forget it.

Then there are those of us who do see our addictions quite clearly and, as a result, we live in a state of intermittent or perpetual self-reproach. We may even work, and work hard, on these patterns, striving to control or tame them. Why? Does it serve any purpose to punish ourselves in this way?

Let's look to Zoey for an answer. Surely she doesn't reproach herself. "Oh no, I've done it again. Why can't I leave mom's clogs alone?! She really likes these Dansko's, and now look, they're *separated*." What's more… "What a weak dog I am. I knew I was about to do this, I knew it was bad, but did I stop myself? Noooo." Remarkably, Zoey is entirely free of such logic.

She's got a point. And so, by way of practice, I've taken to maintaining a sense of humor, of lightness, about sweets. That whole, giant, currant scone? Seriously?? Oh, well, there I go again… better luck next time. And I give credit to enjoyment, to pleasure. Was it good? Oh *yeah*.

I have, for a few years now, worked a full-time job at a university twelve miles from our home. The commute, from one smallish college town to a larger city boasting a rival university, is punctuated by easily a dozen stoplights; multiple turns and exchanges direct a steady stream of motivated drivers from one throughway to another. Twice per day, my strategy for using this otherwise wasted half hour is to listen to CDs, ones carefully chosen to help move me along in my personal and/or spiritual growth. In one of my favorites, with the promising title of "Getting Unstuck," Pema Chodron talks about addictions, from the big and calamitous to the small and ordinary, the stuff of our daily habits. They are not mysterious, she says. "Anyone can create an addiction, it's easy. Just take a hot bath before bed for a week, and then one night tell yourself, 'I'm not going to do that tonight.'" (Laughter, the kind that flows from self-recognition, erupts in the workshop audience.) Apparently, we have some agency over this matter, this question of habit and its darker gradation, addiction.

And so, I set for myself an experiment. Maybe I could decide to select my personal addiction, make it pleasurable and good, and keep it under wraps, while maintaining an attitude of the carefree about it. What will it, this chosen addiction, be? The answer, the obvious one, was... triple-dipped, dark chocolate, Brazil nuts. But of course.

The next weekend, filled with bold purpose, I climbed into my green Honda, journeyed the easy one mile drive to our local gourmet shop, and strolled straight to the candy counter, undistracted by exotic coffees, not even swerving toward the samples that beckoned to me, personally, from tiny wrappers and tastefully arranged platters. At $12.95 per pound, the particular items I had targeted were not to be self-dispensed by the customer; instead, I had to place my request. "Can I please have seven of the Brazils?" This drew a quick look, askance. "*Seven?*" Well, yes. I explained: If I get seven, I have one every day for the week, but if I get a bag with some random number, well, I don't think they'll last through tonight. Full disclosure seemed in order.

The experiment turned out to be a stunning success. I am now the pleased, though not exactly proud, custodian of a triple-dipped, dark chocolate, Brazil nut addiction. One per night. Or else. About this, I can absolutely chuckle.

In playing with addiction, practicing the intentional creation and indulgence of it, (and I acknowledge that I'm fortunate to have just a light touch, a manageable experience, and not full-blown, life-shaping disease), I've noticed something interesting. By appreciating the *positive* side of my addictions, the enjoyment, say, or the relative silliness of the whole situation, I can neutralize a host of negativity – the judgments I make and tend about what seems like weakness of character, or worse, my own slide into self-indulgence. No, I tell myself, I'm not caught in a compulsive pattern. I am managing my anxiety. I'm nurturing myself, even. I'm doing something that soothes me. And hey, as coping strategies go, didn't I choose a good one?

Having flipped the valence with which I view my habits, from negativity and judgment to observation, humor, and playfulness (what goes for positive), I'm now ready to take the next step in my relationship to my various attachments – I'm ready to choose my "shoes" more selectively. Will this one benefit me, support my health (or at least not damage it), affirm my worthiness to enjoy life, make me feel good, allay my restlessness?

And what *is* this restlessness, this unsettled feeling, this neediness – the root of the addiction? I have long thought there's something wrong with me, something that requires work, effort, change. But maybe it's not a defect. Maybe, just maybe, it's the energy that pushes me to take that first step toward finding peace.

3

I've learned a lot about walking from Zoey. Though walking, just walking, may seem like a simple act, its lack of complexity does not give us license to perform it unawares, take it for granted, or fail to dwell in its wonders. What have I learned? First of all, walking involves all of the senses. Second, at its best, it takes no account of time. Third, it unleashes spontaneity, even in the leashed. And perhaps most importantly, its purpose is not function, but pleasure.

For many years, I thought walking was an excellent form of exercise, as well as a golden opportunity to socialize with friends while doing something good for the body. Though it never substituted for what I considered "real" exercise (that is, some form of heart-thumping cardiovascular workout, a designation reserved for activities like running and swimming), walking has held its place in my daily life since my college years. College, almost by definition, is a place where you walk to absolutely everything. Walking becomes the connector that links any and all activities on campus, separating classes, meals, times spent in the dorm, dances, social events. I was fortunate enough to attend a college renowned for its beautiful "country club" grounds, with century-old trees, large green spaces, shrubs and landscaping. Academic gothic dormitories and lecture halls, of brownstone or dark gray granite, formed dignified quads around lovely courtyards, sliced diagonally by paths well worn by countless students' feet. Streets and cars were routed around the periphery, so they did not intrude on the setting's serenity. Walking from here to there gave a pulse to my days, and created an outdoor break, a breather between one thing and another, to quell the intensity of academia.

After graduating from college, I continued to lead a pedestrian life – now in Boston, where a car is more a liability than an asset. Each morning, at the early edge of the commuting hour, I walked from my three-way shared apartment to the subway stop, and on the other end, from a subway stop to a downtown office in the pedestrian-friendly waterfront area, Faneuil Hall. On my way home, another ride on "the T" and a short walk delivered me to the jazz dance studio, and afterward, sweaty and happy, I walked to a T stop in Back Bay, on and off the subway, and home to my apartment. Unlike in college, my shoes rarely touched actual earth. City walking, which connected person with pavement or concrete, was a step removed from the natural – but I was, nonetheless, walking, grounding myself in the regular pattern of my days.

After six good years of living and walking in California, I made my home in the South, in North Carolina to be specific, with my two small children. In this part of the country, and particularly in the context of a young family, embedded in a predominantly suburban culture, walking becomes less of a given. Unlike Berkeley, Oakland, or the older Northeastern cities which grew up around cobblestone streets intended for foot traffic and horse-drawn carriages, Southern towns were born in the Age of the Car. They typically lack an inner, pedestrian-friendly core, nor are they laced with sidewalks or criss-crossed by public transit.

Southerners drive to everything. Driving is, quite simply, a way of life, not questioned or even noticed as a behavior that one might, legitimately, question. Alarmed by this basic and, to my mind, ugly truth about the local lifestyle, I set down a firm precondition for any house that my husband and I might consider buying when we moved to Chapel Hill, namely, I had to be able to walk to things, to get by foot from home to shops, groceries, the public library, the kids' schools, maybe a café, and safely.

Much to my relief, my husband acceded to this condition and we bought our house accordingly. But babies, at times, are less understanding than adult partners. I now had to squeeze my walks, something I considered a birthright, in around the more pressing priorities of feeding, napping, preschool drop-off and pick-up, snacks, and yes, diapering. Even more problematic than the strictures of these schedules, which largely determined *when* I could walk, was the fact that *how* my walks went (peacefully, or with frequent interruptions, or very swiftly and aborted, if high-volume complaints were waged) and even *whether* or not they could happen, now depended on the willingness of small beings – with opinions of their own. For the most part, my desires prevailed, and the walks continued.

Time marched on, delivering my children, though still very young, into what we rather grandiosely call "school," even at the level of morning-out programs and preschool. As they headed out tentatively into their own micro-worlds, along came that most marvelous of creatures, Zoey. Zoey, who never questioned the need for, or desirability of, a walk. In fact, the mere word "walk" sends her into quivery raptures. In Zoey's presence, to manage expectations, we spell out the word – "W - A - L - K -"– unless we plan to deliver immediately on the joyous implicit promise. Sometimes we simply call it a "W." ("Are you guys ready to take Zoey for a W with me?," I might ask, suspecting that the answer would be no, or yes but lacking in near-term follow-through.) After all, we don't want to raise her hopes for nothing.

In the past day or so, Zoey has begun to limp, ever so slightly. I seem to be the only one who notices the almost imperceptible hitch in her step. It saddens me terribly, as the first visible indication in a downhill slide. This tumor, I know, will soon erect a barricade between her and a primary pleasure, walking.

My son, Sam, used to walk Zoey with me first thing in the morning, before school (his) and work (mine). When he reached the strapping, energy-packed age of nine, just after his dad moved out, we began jogging the one-third mile loop around our neighborhood. The pre-breakfast timing made sense in several respects. It was efficient, in that it accomplished exercise for Zoey, Sam, and me in a short burst. It minimized the time we left Carolyn, now only seven, alone in the house. It got Sam, a bit sluggish at 6:30 a.m., up and moving so that, on our return, he was ready to mobilize for the school day. And it fit the time constraints of my schedule as a mom and commuter.

Not a morning person by nature, Zoey complied without complaint. Given her "druthers," however, she would have preferred to actually walk, which would have allowed her the latitude to take in any late-breaking scents, investigate fascinating developments such as, say, a fresh piece of litter on the sidewalk, and carefully select the optimal location for her pit stop. Rather unsympathetically, tugging gently at her leash and nagging at her to move along, I often called her "Lazypaws," an endearment peppered with a dose of impatience.

Zoey, who came equipped with her own ideas about walking, was never swayed by my alternate priorities. Her resolute certainty about what is important, *interesting*, about a walk positioned her as a master teacher, one capable of gently but effectively pressing me to observe and question my pace.

Above all, Zoey likes to stop and sniff. Most likely, these aroma-infused stops provide her with a wealth of information about who has been where, and when. We can only imagine how she reads the scene. Can she tell which, specifically, of her peers were at this precise spot? how long ago? what the dogs had eaten or drunk in the recent past? how they were feeling? whether they were healthy or sick? and importantly, what their owners had been cooking? Surely there is a vast store of information available through the canine nose but hidden from us humans. Thus while dogs become educated, we become impatient. "Not a sniffy tour, Zoey" became my line to nudge her along on our morning jogs. Doesn't she know that Sam needs time to eat his breakfast, that I need to pull on my skirt and nylons? Isn't she itching to get to her own food bowl? Doesn't she, too, feel a twinge of guilt at leaving Carolyn home alone, as we make this circuit? In a word, no.

Zoey leaves me no choice but to accept her simplicity. Her tasks are defined for her in a moment-by-moment way. A bush? Stop, sniff, mark. Another bush? same. A leaf pile? Reams of data worthy of a long stop. A breeze? Ears perked, body fully alert, attention totally focused on this new source of information. And what am I doing? Rushing, allowing my mind to yank me into the future, thinking my way headlong into the day, and thus missing this richness of the moment. In this way, I invite stress.

Novelty, to a dog, is a meaningless concept. It's all new, all novel. I defy you to find a dog who gets bored. They are, quite simply, immune to this experience. Why? We might claim that it's due to their exquisite sensitivity to minutia, their keen sense of smell, for instance, but this lets us off the hook a bit too easily. We humans actually have the capacity for some impressively fine-toothed perception, but we use it infrequently, and even more rarely do we appreciate and cultivate it. Sometimes we use it, but unwisely, harmfully.

For a brief period in my work life, I knew a German biomedical researcher, Gunther, whose specific field was, to those of us not working in the basic sciences, unusual. He spent his days, months, and years studying the sodium ion channels in the neural circuitry of earthworms. Insights would, ultimately and without doubt, shed light on human sensation – in particular, the regulation of thirst. I had assisted this scientist with a funding proposal or two, the mere act of which apparently indicated my interest in his work (possibly a rare occurrence, and one to be capitalized upon). This, in turn, led him to initiate a handful of evening get-togethers. I'm not actually sure if these events were dates or just shared dinners; such ambiguity may be a downside of relations with a hard-core scientist – though to be fair, I lack sufficient evidence to say for sure.

Anyway, Gunther was somewhat straight-faced, and somewhat proper, but exceptionally nice. Other than his science, which was of noted (if niche) significance, he had a feature of which he was quite proud. He could identify wines. On one occasion, over a surprisingly delicious glass of Gewurtztraminer, he related a victorious moment. He had been "at university" at the time, in his home country.

His mentor, a distinguished professor, and several students including Gunther were lingering late over a number of bottles of wine. (This number remained undisclosed.) A challenge went up: Who had the most discerning palate for wine? Gunther was confident, and pegged himself against his mentor, a vintner and owner of a well-stocked cellar. The wine steward arrived with a mystery bottle, cloaked in a plain white cloth right up to the cork. Glasses were poured, carefully maintaining the bottle's anonymity, "bouquets" were wafted, and sips taken. With a swift "Chateaux Something-or-Otheur, 1977," Gunther beat the professor to the punch. The table fell silent as the wine steward unveiled the label. Correct! Even in the retelling, Gunther glowed in the moment's glory.

Yes, even we humans (like dogs) are capable of impressive discernment, of appreciating marvelously thin-sliced detail. We have to cultivate it, but when we do, the ability can give us such depths of pleasure. We, too, can experience the alchemy of fascination and satisfaction we see in our furry friends when they're absorbed in a good scent.

A short, tottering figure approached as Zoey and I walked along the narrow street that paralleled the shore of a tiny lake, more like a pond, and a prime asset of our neighborhood. Looking down between 1970s-style contemporary houses, well-shaded by mature trees, we could see water shimmering in the end-of-day sunlight. He, the owner of one of the lakeshore houses, wore slippers and socks that extended halfway up his thin calves, an elderly man, balding, the weakness of age showing through his ribbed white tank-top undershirt, but his eyes sparkling. "Why is it?" he began, more as though delivering a proclamation than asking a question. "Why is it that women like to paint their bones?" I had to stop and think a minute. Paint their bones? "Put colors on their fingernails, their toenails, all these tattoos you see nowadays…" Ah, well.

"Women aren't like men," I hazarded, keeping fairly safe for starters. "Mostly they don't compare themselves as much on performance as on looks, so they've come up with all these ways to differentiate themselves, to refine their appearances." He smiled, as if I had just described some child's antics, and gave me the context for his musings. He had just returned from the local nail salon, where he had been the only male. (I give him credit for going!) "My daughter-in-law thought I needed to take better care of myself, so she got me one of those gift certificates…" The experience had mystified him – all this attention, all this expense, to put colors on one's nails. "They get a lot of encouragement," I assured him, half-heartedly defending my kind, and after a disclaimer (I have never had a manicure), launching into a mini-diatribe about the fashion industry, how it thrives on creating needs, how it teaches women to evaluate themselves based on appearance, and then to drill down to ever finer levels of detail. And, on a roll, I pointed out that women kind of have to do this, to try to look good. Studies have shown that people, if shown two pictures of women, will attribute greater intelligence, a more agreeable personality, and various other positive attributes to the one who is, yes, prettier. So much for fairness.

"I find there's another sort of discrimination that no one pays any attention to," said my neighbor. "I'm five foot six and for a man, that's really short. I've battled discrimination based on my height for my whole entire life." This is a man who attended Harvard University and Medical School, pursued a successful, lengthy career in Medicine, has traveled extensively, partaken of all the finest aspects of our culture, and yet, has suffered at the hands of his reviewers – by their judgment.

"Ridiculous," I agreed, shaking my head. A tug on the leash reminded me that we'd kept Zoey waiting long enough. We each went on our way, returning to our respective worlds, though separated by several decades, both measured in myriad ways by the fine-toothed demarcations that separate us from others, from those near to us and from others unknown but envisioned in a general sense, and ultimately from our selves.

In recent years I've begun to consider my walks as Soul Time. I don't just look at the sky, I really *see* it in all its depth, blueness, expansiveness, its incomprehensible beauty. I marvel as something miraculous happens in the theater of its boundless dome: twice every day, the sky morphs from one color to the next, traversing through innumerable shades and hues, presenting ever-shifting patterns of color and overlays of texture. Amazing! I hear birds, really *hear* them for the music they create, sometimes a symphony, sometimes a solo performance, and at times, usually in the peak of spring when territories and mates are at a premium, a cacophony. I could go on, but the point is that I see, surrounding me, gift after gift. They appear effortlessly, not for the asking but merely presenting themselves for the receiving. The more I look, the more I realize that it's *all* gift, this wonder of a life we swim in, like clear cool waters of awareness, of blessing. And so, these days, I find myself thanking God for the gift of another day with my Zoey.

I was once related, through marriage, to a woman who was fundamentally pragmatic. It is possible that she was starry-eyed or whimsical as a girl, that she had romantic fantasies and idealistic visions, but if these ever existed, they had long since departed by the time I entered upon her family's scene. Now she prides herself on her steady grasp of "reality," her sensible approach to nearly everything. She talks politics and current events, rather than personal challenges and aspirations. Her day, every day, begins with a cup of coffee prepared in identical fashion (instant, with half-and-half, no sugar), over which she completes (yes, completes) the *New York Times* crossword puzzle, unaided by any crossword "dictionary" or similar instrument of cheating and, impressively, in pen. When her husband died quite unexpectedly in his early sixties, this woman was left with a very comfortable cushion of assets. Immediately, she turned to travel.

During their marriage, her husband, even more the pragmatist than she, had held the reins with respect to travel, confining their destinations to hiking meccas that were both economical and beautiful, all of them located in North America. Now Turkey beckoned. Novelty, rather than natural beauty, became her mission, her principal decision-making criterion. And, unlike her husband, she was not a born walker. After she had completed several guided tours, each to a different exotic land, I asked her what dreams lay ahead, what next trips. She turned the question back to me, "Do you have any suggestions?" "Switzerland?" I proposed, assuming a dreamy look, seeing in my mind's eye a high alpine meadow rimmed by snow-covered peaks, bespeckled with wildflowers, cowbells clinging in the distance. With a rare, almost conspiratorial, intimacy she brushed off my suggestion, "Frankly, Jane, been there, done that." She, this woman who lives in the same world as I, the same country even, must inhabit a different universe.

An insomniac since my teenage years, I've only recently become able to "sleep in" on weekends. This, I acknowledge, is a relative term; my victory is sleeping until, say, somewhere between 6:00 and 7:00 a.m., before popping out of bed. This new practice lends an air of indulgence to the weekend, though one which I'm a bit embarrassed to mention. Recently, I have extended this decadence (in which, obviously, I need further practice) to encompass the Dog Walk.

And so, I've begun coaching myself, on weekends when I can afford the time, to walk around the block at Zoey's pace. What luxury to release my grip on measured time, to adopt her way of padding not along a timeline, but through a matrix of time, a richly textured mesh. Moving at her speed, I catch a glimpse of what she experiences – the freshness that wafts each day through this daily routine, a track either of us could surely, by this point, retrace with our eyes shut. I am aware of how much more her senses pick up than mine, and honor her for these mysterious capacities. I can only wonder what makes this rock or that bush smell so, well, fascinating.

But who holds the trump is far from clear. I am simultaneously aware that I can tune into something for which Zoey has no concept – my Soul. Here in the outdoors, alone with my dog, walking, I can talk to my self, without even the crutch of silent words. And I can listen for the wordless knowing, the wisdom that doesn't need to be expressed, that doesn't come in response to mental churning or thoughts, that doesn't predict or react or explain. Wisdom arrives fortuitously in the empty spaces.

Against the backdrop of this conversation with Soul, exercise, the original and still ostensible purpose of the Dog Walk, becomes not trivial but, simply, fortuitous.

4

Zoey is a girl with a taste for luxury. She's unabashed, shameless, in her pursuit of the poofiest pillow, the cushiest cushion, the fluffiest comforter. She prefers goose down.

The down, in our house, comes courtesy of my mother, a Maine native who has long felt that her North Carolina-residing daughter does a poor job of preparing herself or her family for warmth in winter. She observes that going to college at a quasi Southern school (to a full-blooded Yankee, New Jersey is barely above the Mason-Dixon Line), living several years in Northern California, and now spending over a decade in Chapel Hill, have wiped out not only my adaptive skills, but also my common sense. And my winter wardrobe. These various gaps all become most clearly evidenced in my failure to dress appropriately for the cold.

Pragmatism marks a full-blooded Yankee, as surely as nervousness marks a Chihuahua or good-naturedness a Golden Retriever. And so, my mother takes matters into her own hands. She scoffs at our thin cotton sweaters which, for performance, can't compete with wool. Determined that someone should manage the demands of climate in a sensible way, she buys warm winter coats for my children each year, to shield them from the potentially biting cold on our weeklong Christmas visit to New England. She insists that the kids wear garments that are largely alien to Southerners – hats, mittens, scarves, snow pants. And, to my delight, she has sent two soft and cozy down comforters. Intended, of course, for use by her two grandchildren. Zoey and I were not in line for receiving: I, as her daughter, should know by now how to manage for myself the cold of night-time, and Zoey, well, since my mother was not one to adopt trendy concepts such as "grand dog," she received not even a passing thought.

Zoey has a quiet way of simultaneously asserting her doggy preferences and filling her personal needs. To her own reasoning, she does not need to ask permission. Without shame or guilt over her physical pleasures, she simply makes a choice – goose down wins out, over the other options available in our household. She knows cotton; she's flirted with fleece; but it's down that entices her to settle upon it at bedtime. She makes no apologies for occupying my down pillow, flattening my down comforter with her body weight, making a dent in my featherbed after I have fluffed it for myself. I suppose we share this penchant for softness in the evening.

When I was sixteen, I left home for "early college" in western Massachusetts. In the throes of teenage angst and self-loathing, I was desperate to get away from emotional pressures I couldn't even define, let alone articulate or understand. They manifested, largely, in attacks on my self, in self-denigration and self-denial. Looking back, I seemed bent on proving my unworthiness not just to myself but also to the world around me. While my peers were exploring their own attractiveness, I was despairing at my utter lack thereof. It would be decades before, for instance, I allowed myself to experiment with eye liner, much less mascara or, alarmingly, eye shadow. While my friends were taking steps to claim – even flaunt – their newfound femaleness, I did my best to stomp mine out. To their halter tops and mini skirts (this was the seventies, after all), I wore long sleeves and long pants. I was ashamed, not, as they were, hesitantly proud, of my shape.

My self-critique was multi-dimensional. I cultivated a harsh inner taskmaster, forcing myself to work inordinately hard at everything I did. Everything took on the serious tenor of a frantic struggle to be good enough – at flute, school, tennis, running. I lost weight which, of course, made me look and feel worse. I was, in fact, a psychological wreck. Completely absent from my personal compass was any concept of physical pleasure, of worthiness to enjoy.

And then I arrived at Simon's Rock Early College, assigned to live at the end of a hallway (upgraded by the school's lexicon to "suite") housing twenty-odd girls who had similarly been misfits in their own high school environments. Fortunately, I landed on a dorm floor that was cohered into a community by "Mellen" (a contraction of Maryellen which her friends loved and family detested), a warm, empathic, utterly supportive and caring Resident Advisor. She was all of twenty years old, an advanced age which I assumed conferred perspective and wisdom. Mellen's influence blended our tremendous diversity, for we all came to Simon's Rock driven part by talent and part by maladjustment, into a place where my hallmates and I called each other "suities," where the intention to value one another was explicit. We regularly exchanged backrubs; hugs were the normal mode of greeting. Over many a cup of Celestial Seasonings tea, Roastaroma or Lemon Zinger, swizzled with honey and drunk in stoneware mugs, we bared our hearts and souls to each other. In frequent gatherings, held impromptu in each others' rooms at all hours of day and night, we sang Crosby, Stills, Nash, and Young songs, or Cat Stevens, or Peter, Paul, and Mary, one of us strumming an acoustic guitar. The iceberg of my inner world began to melt, ever so slightly.

Among these new friends, our first affirmations of our own self-worth may have looked, to parents or other evaluators, like acts of defiance. We quit wearing bras, shaving our legs, eating meat, using deodorant. But for me, rather than a departure *from*, this signified a coming *to*. To what? I had unwittingly joined a new culture.

We refused to indulge ourselves, a statement which for many amounted to taking a stance against the Establishment, against privilege and materialism. I, myself, had mastered this no-frills concept as a way of punishing and rejecting myself. But here, the acts of non-indulgence took on a positive, self-affirming character wholly unfamiliar, even antithetical, to me. Just post-sixties, we were coasting on the end of the hippy era, creating our own personal variants of the flower child and buildling, intentionally, a community. We sang, together. We made brownies, not with chocolate (politically incorrect) but with carob, together. We lounged together, for no particular reason other than to be in each others' company. We burned candles and incense, and hung Indian tapestries on our walls. We walked and talked, together. My iceberg melted a bit more.

But still I remained my toughest critic, and an unremitting personal slave-driver. Though I was starting to learn to connect, tentatively and with only partial trust, the concept of self-nurturance still sat well beyond the horizon. I had first to master self-acceptance, a task that would take me another couple decades. So, through college and graduate school, I succeeded in rising to meet measurable expectations – grades, degrees, accomplishments, jobs – at the expense of taking care of myself, at least, that is, of doing so *with kindness*. For I could make myself eat healthy foods, go to bed and get up at the right times, exercise, but there was no laxity, no freedom or choice, and thus not much pleasure, in these disciplines. They were just that, discipline, rather than self *care*. Later on, marriage even became an exercise in denial of my self. As if scripted, I found a mate who gladly shouldered the burden, with me, not of growing together in love and exploration, but of holding me on the judgment block, of denying my luxurious feminine essence. This, I suppose, was the best I could do at the time; it was familiar, actionable, within my comfort zone.

Zoey was a mere youngster when I asked my ex-husband to leave. She supported me in this extreme, triumphant, unprecedented affirmation of self-worth. For I had finally and irreversibly come to the point where I could say, "I don't deserve this." And even more importantly, "I deserve better." What accounted for this shift, a discontinuity of sorts, this sudden ability to take a bold step toward my self, toward actually *caring* for my self?

I can't explain how. What arrived, somehow, mysteriously, was a knowing, a sensation at the core of my being that I experienced as a gradual dawn of certainty. This was a startling experience for one who, characteristically, was not certain about much of anything. My usual tactic is to scan the room for clues as to how others perceive something, for indications of how they would respond, and then, only then, to formulate an idea of what I know. But this time, concerning the end of my marriage, I *knew* the action that I needed to take, and I knew it *within myself,* not because of what others told me or what I guessed they would think.

With this knowing came a stark realization about the challenge that we call Life, a realization that threw me back into full reliance on myself, but that did so without engendering a sense of abandonment, aloneness, or failure. Let me tell you this lesson: It is that self-love is one of our hardest, but also one of our most significant, assignments in this school we call Life. It's far easier to loathe, than it is to love, one's Self. In fact, there's a perverse self-indulgence in self-loathing; it keeps us totally absorbed in our troubles, mired in our deficiencies, involved with our self. And so, paradoxically, there is more pride entwined with self-deprecation and self-hatred than there is in true self-love, which is not self-aggrandizing but rather an honest inward kindness that knows, understands, and accepts.

Consider Zoey, a pup without artifice. She never questions her own deservingness, her entitlement to physical comforts, the raw pleasure she finds in taking care of herself. You might say that she expresses a perfect acceptance, a love of her own beingness as she knows it. She has needs; she has desires; and though aware of these, she has no pride.

So I've learned to do the most simple of actions. I take baths, bubble baths, mineral soaks, hot and foamy. I settle into the warmth and say, "ahhh." Out loud. My daughter finds this a bit silly, but, well, that's mom. I luxuriate in my soft bed, and affirm, "mmmm, this is *good*." I light candles, at the dinner table and in my bedroom, though no one but me will be there to appreciate them. When my children are with their father for a weekend, I buy myself salmon and make a love feast. Yes, by myself and for myself. Whose responsibility is this, if not mine? Who, but me, will cultivate the love within me, and if that love within is not nourished and nurtured, how can it radiate outward?

This is, clearly, my work. The stakes are high, but so is the pay-off – accruing for others, true, since our well-being and happiness have endless ripple-out effects, but primarily benefiting myself because, hmmm, I suppose just because I am. This is my work, and I accept the challenge.

5

Chapel Hill lives up to its name. Flat spaces are few and far between. Mostly, the land heaves and falls as though some giant sculptor, working from beneath, had scooped it out in places and lumped it up in others. The pattern, if present at all, is whimsically random, steep rises and precipitous drop-offs interspersed with gentle undulation. Water, following its intrinsically fluid and adaptive nature, conforms to the contours of the land. And so, in its lower parts, the town is laced by creeks. Our neighborhood, Oxford Hills, backs up to one of these, a wiggly rock-strewn path of water that moves sometimes slow and sleepy, and at other times, after a sudden storm or a day of steady rain, rushing and thunderous. Always, however, it is a mild chocolate brown.

Under a canopy of sweet gums, locusts, poplars, and pines, a forest of dense and dark green in the summer that becomes a thick tangle of bare branches and vines in the winter, a bike path meanders, roughly tracing the course of the creek. And along this, yesterday, I came across my neighbor, Tanya. We were both walking our dogs, as it was lovely weather for early February. The fresh air washed across my face and through my lungs, cleaning out my inner spaces and my weary mind, cluttered from a morning spent in front of the computer.

Tanya's dog, Polo, is a fixture in my life. Every day after work, because my work-day ends far earlier than hers, I walk Polo along with Zoey, up to the playground and then back again, trailed by a half dozen elementary schoolers. And so, every day, I see the inside of Tanya's house, as if a window into a foreign land, her world. The glimpse of her life is intimate: breakfast and perhaps last night's supper dishes in the kitchen sink (usually take-out); tennis shoes hastily removed, likely after an intense match at the faculty club; unopened mail and newspapers on the table, too little time to tackle them on a busy weeknight. Despite this view behind the stage, I rarely see Tanya herself. And since our paths so rarely cross, she didn't know about the cancer.

It seems wrong, somehow, to call it "Zoey's cancer." This invader, this disease, is not of her choosing; she does not, most definitely does not, own it; rather, *it* is waging a war to own her. It has taken up residence, alien, unbidden, not *of* her though undeniably *in* her.

Commiserating with my distress, Tanya confided that Polo, whom she loves dearly, has a heart murmur. This, she informed me, she has decided to ignore. The conversation slid effortlessly from these confidences into a favorite litany of the Dog Owner, namely, the unconditional nature of a dog's love. Our dogs, who greet us exuberantly after even our worst days at work, who depend on us, who accept whatever we can give and forgive us for our negligence when we are just plain too busy, who look at us with trusting, soulful eyes. It's no wonder we love them beyond measure.

"I don't know what I would do without Polo," Tanya muses, almost visibly holding despair at arm's length. This question, for me, is no longer rhetorical. Falling now uncomfortably within the category of the literal, it is not one I like to even consider. Zoey provides a free flow of love in our house; she's forthcoming with comfort and support, in her canine way; she doesn't judge, reprimand, or censure us; she reveres and defers to us; she loves us thoroughly. But unconditionally?

Just this fall, Zoey, my loving companion and the supposed source of unconditional love, bit me. It was a serious bite, one with purpose, and emphatically not just a nip. She meant it.

Events of the autumn had taken their toll on both me and Zoey. For my part, I was frazzled from life with an alternately angry, belligerent, and depressed teenager. On this particular afternoon, I was talking on the phone with my parents, once again plying their patience by describing, at (probably interminable) length, my difficulties managing Sam's violent adolescent outbursts. His rage once again had culminated in a hole punched in the drywall, not to mention bloody knuckles. My nerves were frayed, my serenity rattled.

As we talked, I multi-tasked, scrubbing dishes at the kitchen sink, wiping crumbs and stray sesame seeds, remnants of toasted bagels, from the counters. Through the cloud of my distraction, a strange thumping noise broke into my consciousness. For a moment, it hovered on the outskirts of awareness, and for that moment, I floated in a state of non-action, much as you might tolerate an alarm clock beeping for several minutes before suddenly, sharply, becoming aware, then awake, enough to turn it off. Something had happened upstairs! I dashed around the corner of the kitchen, through the living area, and up the two short flights of stairs to my daughter's bedroom.

There was Zoey, defiantly staring up at me amid a scene of general bedroom wreckage. Aspen chips strewn about the carpet, the shrapnel of a disaster involving small pet rodents. Using every ounce of her twenty-five-pound terrier strength, Zoey had pulled Carolyn's two pet rats, wire mesh cage and all, off of the low table that served as stand, onto the floor, and halfway across her room. From the disarray in the rats' cage and surrounding it, I discerned that Zoey had rolled the cage over at least one time, and probably more. The horror of it struck me hard. What had this been like for Annabelle and Eloise? Terrifying. Atrocious treatment for our newest family members, adorable youngsters, whom I had given as a birthday present to Carolyn on her recent thirteenth.

On top of the parenting nightmares I had just related to my parents, this catastrophe was just too much to take. And on top of this, my protective juices, the mama bear in me, reared tall. I hate to admit it, but I reacted immediately and from my gut. I yelled at Zoey. Loud. Worse still, I whacked her. And within a millisecond, she bit me.

Unconditional love? Something had been lost in translation. At that moment, with my hand a mass of blood, I could find scarcely a trace of the purported unconditional love within this dog, my own. "You *bit* me!" I wailed, sobbing with the pain, but even more so, with dismay. How could you?! You, who love me unconditionally? It *hurts*. Earlier I was stretched to the breaking point by my son's troubles, but managing to hold myself together, to function. Now my tears flowed at this betrayal or, at least equally distressing and probably more, this abandonment.

People use the term "container" these days to talk about a safe space for discussion, for processing of thoughts and feelings, for interacting when the stakes are high. To me, the word says Tupperware. Let's be more specific: In a business context, people certainly do need protection from retaliation, they need shelter from harsh office politics, a psychologically safe space in which they can speak their minds and be heard without retribution, when appropriate. But a container? It seems they need the opposite, something more like freedom than containment. For if the safety they seek is contained, what happens when they exit the container, when they return to the real world outside the container walls, but still engaged with the same people who joined them within those guardrails? Could be risky.

In the personal context, it can be equally – or more – unsafe to air our emotions, though we may need to just to keep our souls breathing. In emotionally rough times, we long for an oasis where our feelings can be present without being judged, essentially, we long for a place of unconditional love. Is this a container? It seems more like a womb, a haven that is pregnant with the possibilities of growth, a future, new life. The image exudes warmth, nurturance, and protection.

A container breaks. If made of plastic, it becomes brittle with age, eventually cracking so that it no longer holds its contents; if glass, it can shatter, spilling all. But a womb, too, provides only transient safety; its destiny is to burst, not randomly but at the precise time when we are matured to the point of readiness. When the womb breaks, we have not ruin and waste, but birth, a new reality into which we have grown.

You may wonder why I am not embarrassed to recount that, throughout childhood and adolescence, I called my grandmother "Gaga." I'll go even further and confess that we, my three siblings and I, all of us in our forties, still refer to her this way. Quite simply, the name fits – perhaps not matching the person, for how could anyone over the age of one really fit this moniker, but aligning with the aura.

Gaga, known to the rest of her world as Florence, had grown up in the roaring twenties. I remember a sepia-toned photo of her, in flapper garb, wearing a hat and drop-waste dress, glancing coyly over her shoulder at the camera. She lived through the Great Depression and World War II, sheltered by her prosperous maritime family living in Salem, Massachusetts. She was Yankee to a fault: She saved scrupulously – twist ties and rubber bands, S&H green stamps, pennies kept in jars, small bottles with a tablespoon of, say, mint jelly in the fridge; nothing went to waste. Even to my young ears, she had an accent which shone through in words like "hoss" (horse), "con" (corn), and lobstuh. She painted, mostly pictures of the rocky Maine coast where she lived, the ocean in storms and calm, and her family, all eleven grandchildren. She bustled tirelessly about her house, a large, dark brown shingled, ark-like home set well back from the cliff, always busying herself with those household tasks so mysterious to a child. She doted on her rock garden, peppered with shells washed up from the North Atlantic. Her unique constellation of eccentricities, tendencies and talents, loves and lore, combined to make her, in our minds, Gaga.

In our childhood world of danger, the threat of harsh emotions around every corner in our own home, with the ever-present possibility of our mother's rage erupting, Gaga provided refuge. We spent many a long weekend, school vacation, or summer holiday at her house. And every time, as we piled out of the car, pent up after driving from our home in Massachusetts to hers in Maine, she would be at the door, waiting. Bell buoys clanged in the background as she welcomed us. Invariably, she had baked cookies (ranger cookies were a specialty) and often bread – white bread, all the more delicious for being taboo in our own house. She wore an apron, an integral component of her enveloping hug. She used nicknames ("Janey," music to my endearment-starved ears), asked a minimum of questions, played Kings in the Corner and checkers with us, but mostly, she provided a backdrop of acceptance, regardless of whatever our family was doing (walking on the beach, rock-hopping at the lighthouse, skiing). There was no need, no cause, to question her love.

After leaving home in my mid-teens, time exerted its transformative powers on both me and Gaga. I was growing up, distancing myself from my family, finding my own path. I rarely saw her, though I heard about the slow creep of Alzheimer's, the progression from large house on the coast to condo, then nursing home. I visited a handful of times, with my mother, and found myself awkward, ill-equipped, not knowing what to do or say. Gone was the person I had known, whose support I had cherished but taken for granted; in her place was just a body, one with baffling responses. She talked, but this "she" was not Gaga. She ate, but not like herself. She sat up, though she didn't move around like a conscious person. To my mother, she had become "a shell."

It is the nature of Life to change. We don't always like this. As babies, we enter the world kicking our tiny legs and wailing, though it's unclear whether in anger or horrified distress. What am I doing here?? Having outgrown our protective womb, we learn that birth into a new way of life is not optional. Our senses expand to take in a larger reality; we breathe new air. And then, along the way from birth to our final transition out of this world, we continue to outgrow the present. Like a snake shedding its skin, allowing the silky under-skin to surface, like a caterpillar bursting forth from its chrysalis, no longer a homely worm but a butterfly, we must, yes we must, let go of the comfortable present in order to be born into a brave new – and potentially beautiful – future.

But as we face change, the unavoidable, where can we find a safe haven for our heart? Is there no choice but to release the wish, the fervent longing, for a reliable sort of love, a love that doesn't morph as everything around it does, an unconditional love? Does change – transition, and the birth it implies – have to entail the death of security, of love as we have known it? In the rushing river of time, we journey across our many (though not all) transitions alone; the bravery required of us is that we dare to jump across the rapids from one stepping stone to the next, leaving the past stone, which may have held us safely for a while, completely behind us in order to move forward to the next, which offers greater stability or brings us closer to shore. We can do this, and at many (though not all) junctures, we must.

Gaga died, peacefully I am told. Was she alone? What did she find, as her spirit made a silent exit from our physical world and a passage to the next phase? I imagine that she entered a womb, metaphorically speaking, a place of unconditional love from which she could be born to a new life.

I married for love, really I did. I imagine we all do. But at twenty-six, I knew very little beyond fairy-tale visions and dreams – idealistic at best, more likely delusional. I, myself, hadn't experienced any such thing as unconditional love, not in my family, from parents or siblings, not from any role models or cherished seniors, not from a god who would, in the first half of my life anyway, have been shaped in the image of what I knew. Nonetheless, I had fantasies, romantic and beautiful ones. I hoped and expected that boundless and unconditional love was the destiny of my marriage.

As a young wife, I did my level best to earn my husband's love, kindness, warmth, and interest. I didn't ask for concern, believing my troubles to be my own, but I did seek to please, to *do* things that would make him love and care for me. I spent hours planning and preparing dinners that I thought he would like, slaved in the kitchen for hours to produce meals – crepes with exotic seafood filling, creamy quiche with flaky crust, variations of the quesadilla that would appeal to his Texan roots. I, a careful vegetarian at the time and lactose intolerant to boot, didn't touch these things. I swept the hardwood and vacuumed the carpets daily, took out the trash and recyclables every Tuesday, washed and folded his laundry on Saturdays, paid the bills. I anticipated his wants and needs. As time went on, I took on more and more of the chores, until eventually I shouldered the full burden of house and yard. I'm not sure now if I looked comical or pathetic, mowing our front yard with a push mower in the 95-degree heat of July and August, keeping one eye on a baby watching from the stroller, while carrying on a conversation with a toddler stacking rocks on the sidewalk. This was, simply, how it was; I didn't question.

Ironically, my efforts did not buy me love, no, they had quite the opposite effect. The harder I worked to earn them, the more elusive became the qualities I sought – the affection, appreciation, closeness. Through all of my fervent and well-intentioned trying, I was sowing the seeds not of great love, but of resentment.

My strategy, in fact, backfired. Rather than padding my account, bankrolling love by delivering more and more service to my husband, my efforts unwittingly repelled him. He came home late, and then later, and then he began returning to work after dinner. He agreed to regular Thursday evening "date nights," one-sidedly arranged by me, on the condition that we not talk about "the relationship." And then, he just simply stopped talking to me. Dinners became a lonely proposition, triangular in geometry, in which we each talked to and with the kids, and only to each other in this indirect way. He opted to sleep in our bonus room, or on the couch, rather than in a shared bed. As the markers of intimacy, of a functioning marriage, dropped away, I felt hurt, unable yet to understand how I had cornered him out.

It took me over ten years to acknowledge that the marriage was effectively dead, that I was stuck in my dread fear, a loveless marriage. My role in this fiasco, the fatal flaw I introduced, lay in my fundamental misunderstanding of the ways of love. Where was the guidebook? I had thought I could gain love by *doing*, that I could earn my husband's heart by actions that filled his needs and nourished his body and soul.

Over the close course of years, I finally woke up to the fact that love arises not from acts of doing, but from ways of being. It bubbles up like a spring from within, rises like mist off a lake at dawn, spreads like the first pink glow of a sunrise. It is apprehended, not made. And I, in my ignorance, had been trying to create it through force of hand – when what was asked of me was merely to step aside, and allow it.

Infuriated and self-defensive, Zoey had acted out. The bite had undeniably stung, on multiple levels. It had shocked me into doubting a basic moral tenet – you do not hurt one whom you love. But her being-ness, her loving devoted presence, returned shortly after this transgression. In fact, in a matter of an hour she seemed to have forgotten that there had been any sort of altercation between us. It was me, and me only, saddened, who harbored a slight bruise on my heart.

I have a confession to make about Zoey, one which I'm ashamed to admit, especially now as she becomes increasingly vulnerable. But, in the spirit of full disclosure, I will tell you: Zoey is a racist. A small and unassuming female in her encounters with other dogs, regardless of their size, heft, or lack thereof, she fancies herself a powerful watchdog when it comes to people. This alter ego is most apparent when she's on home turf; here she reserves her most convincing displays for situations involving clear-cut threat, for instance, a person ringing the doorbell. No matter how complacent and calm she may have been, napping peacefully in her doggie bed, the doorbell causes her to spring instantly to action, tear across the house, skittering on the hard-wood floor of our hallway leading up to the door, and barking with her topmost vigor and volume. The household is immediately catapulted into high alert.

To initiate performance of her role as dedicated Protector of House and Home, Zoey no longer requires an arrival at our literal doorstep. Perception of threat now suffices. She has refined her skills to the point where even a neighbor – presumably a known entity – strolling down the sidewalk in front of our house can alert her to impending danger, triggering her vigilant response. This escalation of her reaction, an innocuous sort of hypersensitivity, looks comical (alternately annoying) in a small dog. In humans, however, it becomes more sinister, as we turn this excessive responsiveness on one another.

For years, we've been on continuous orange alert, always encouraged to "keep our baggage with us at all times," in the airport, public places. Definitely "do not accept items from unknown persons." We install burglar alarms and hire security personnel. Like us, Zoey takes very seriously the inherent threat of intruders, and accepts the attendant responsibility. But unlike us, she also knows how to let it go. Once she has satisfied herself that the danger has past, the potential intruder being now safely a hundred yards or so down the sidewalk and distancing himself further with every step, she casually (sometimes triumphantly) returns to her doggie bed, allowing her system to settle from red alert back down through the rainbow of alarm to a peaceful shade of purple – no threat; serenity is reclaimed.

I have a theory: the unpleasantness of a dog's bark is inversely proportional to the dog's size. Zoey is a small dog, and her bark is, correspondingly, loud and shrill. She wields it with skill, menacing any potential intruder. (Incidentally, my sister disagrees with this theory. The owner of two Papillons, a breed which pretty much defines the term "yappy," she insists that the low and booming bark of a large dog is far worse, in that it is intimidating and scary, not just annoying. True, I acknowledge, but my index measures not the inducement of fear, but the jarring of nerves.) An explosion of barking assaults the senses, and can border on the obnoxious. At times, perhaps to keep safe in a world of ambiguity, Zoey errs on the side of the false positive. This leads her to over-respond, and even to launch her tirade against me, as I unlock the back door, grocery bags perched in one arm, jimmying key in lock with the other hand. Unapologetic, she glibly transitions from barks to licks once the door opens, scarcely an "oops" apparent in her now delighted demeanor. It was a mere case of mistaken identity, I suppose, for which she might feel embarrassed if she were, well, human.

Chapel Hill, located squarely in the Southeastern United States, remains far from racially integrated. Most neighborhoods in our town are either white or Black, though a few are slightly and self-consciously mixed. The determining factors, here like elsewhere in the country, remain most overtly socioeconomic. Our neighborhood is no exception; in our small development, we have only one home that's owned by neighbors of African descent – an erudite couple affiliated with the local university. The other families are all middle class, white collar, and either white/Caucasian or Asian. Scarcely a quarter mile away from this quiet neighborhood, tucked away to the side of the main throughway leading to the downtown area, is a housing project which, I would venture to guess, is one hundred percent Black.

We never see these people, though technically they are our neighbors. On the occasional days when I start my commute a bit late, I drive past a bus stop bustling with elementary school children, all Black. That is pretty much the extent of the diversity I see in and around our community; the others, those who are not middle or upper class and white, shop in different grocery stores, seem not to use the public library, don't show up in the music lessons and swim team practices where I take my kids. Zoey, having a narrower range of motion, almost never sees alternative colors of skin.

Like any home owner, I occasionally call on workmen to help with the ever-changing and sequential needs of my house's deteriorating exterior. First the wood trim and window sills rotted; then the siding turned to mush in places, presenting an inviting opportunity for woodpeckers to excavate in search of bugs; the gutters filled up and overflowed, causing more damage to siding; mildew grew on the north side; and the deck all but fell apart. In these realms, I'm out of my league. With the most recent repairs (involving punky windowsills), much to Zoey's alarm, a team of two Black workmen arrived to give an estimate, negotiate the cost, plan the work, and presumably restore "integrity" to a small portion of my house. One has to start somewhere.

I chose this team of two – Winston, the older man who fulfilled the managerial functions, Jeb the one who climbed the ladder and wielded the hammer – for their apparent honesty and unpretentious, hard-working natures. They were devout Christians, and the fact that their off-hours lives revolved around God and church reassured me. Their arrival with truck and tools was a sight for sore eyes, or in their vernacular, a "blessing"; if you are not "handy," these house issues weigh on you. But for Zoey, the experience of this team was quite the opposite.

Winston and Jeb, I fear, were not Zoey's first encounter with people of color. In my days of walking her and Polo to the elementary school, waiting for the school bell to ring, and leading a parade of kids home, she saw, each day, a flood of newly emancipated children released from the strictures of public education. Many among these kids were Black, residents of the housing projects near our neighborhood and elsewhere around Chapel Hill. Routinely, Zoey growled at them; at those who good-naturedly approached to deliver a pat, she barked furiously. This behavior stood in sharp distinction to her reaction to white children, whom she tolerated quietly, and sometimes humored with a tentative wag of her tail. (She saved her full display of excitement, of course, for "her" children; to others, she maintained a certain aloofness, a natural reserve.) I was ashamed of Zoey's patent racially-defined favoritism, and mortified by the thought that these friendly and well-meaning Black kids, dog lovers even, would be either afraid or hurt by Zoey's prejudice. Fortunately, and much to my relief, I found that young children don't seem to project these sorts of damaging suspicions onto animals. The concept "dog" and the concept "racist" didn't mix.

In more financially endowed days, I had a charming cleaning man, Leon, come to the house on alternate Wednesdays. He focused on, as he called it, the "detail work." Any house with kids needs cleaning more than biweekly, and I expected to do the routine cleaning myself, but the nitty-gritty of bathrooms, kitchen, nooks and crannies lay beyond my capacities.

Leon, a tall, lanky, and friendly Black gentleman who defined the term "dapper," nurtured a mild fear of dogs. He took Zoey's treatment of him rather personally, I fear, and endeavored his noble best to establish a mutually understood truce. Recognizing that he was, after all, in *her* house, Leon tiptoed around Zoey, reassured her that he wasn't going to bother her, and kept a safe distance – all strategies more likely enacted to appease his own fears than hers. Only after numerous visits from Leon did Zoey eventually acclimate to the presence of this threatening being, always respectful and professionally dressed, in her home, but eventually she settled into grudging acceptance. She supervised him closely, but from a distance.

Somewhere along the way, I noticed an interesting twist on Zoey's reactions to the unfamiliar "other" who, to this point, she had defined by race. The observation came about rather by accident.

I, myself, don't wear sunglasses, never have, don't want to, possibly never will. However, I should. In my mid-thirties, I was struck by an ocular malady with an absurd name, pinguecula. This syndrome involves a thickening of a portion of the eyeball, causing a sort of whitish lump on the cornea. I might not have noticed this if pinguecula didn't also involve a small measure of discomfort, somewhere between an itch and low-level pain. Alarmed by something noticeably threatening my eye, that window not only inward to the soul, but outward to the world, I consulted an expert. Pinguecula, the opthalmologist informed me, arises as a protective response on the part of the eye to sunlight. The prescription? I must, thereafter, wear sunglasses anytime I expose my eyes to the sun, the source of all outdoor lighting. Me, who lives to be outside! Clearly this doctor had no concept of the magnitude of challenge he asked of me.

Dutifully, I bought a decent pair of sunglasses and consigned myself to wearing them whenever I went outdoors, or at least, during the sunny times of day. On Day One, preparing to take Zoey out for a walk, I donned the shades. To my great surprise, and adding insult to injury, Zoey growled. She barked. She bristled and backed away. From me! Caught off guard, I whipped off the offending glasses, and stooped to reassure her, a conciliatory hand outstretched. She sniffed my hand, glanced warily at my face, and immediately settled down. I put the sunglasses back on; she resumed her growling. Aha! Well, I didn't like wearing them anyway.

And so, when my friends, Winston and Jeb, come to the door, to paint or hammer or saw, I'm less ashamed of Zoey now. We can chat about our families ("How is your father?," Winston invariably asks me) and the weather (always hotter than any of us remember) while Zoey thunders harmlessly in the background. After all, to her little doggie mind, skin color, sunglasses, who knows what else – these are simply markers of the unfamiliar. She's threatened, not by race, but by the unknown. Who among us isn't, to some degree, whether we openly admit it or hide the evidence in the shelters of emotion? Perhaps we could learn from our dogs about the genesis of racism, or any "ism," about their basis in fear and self-protection and our own smallness. That, I do think, could take us far along the road toward their disempowerment.

7

Ever so slightly, Zoey has started to limp. The mass on her shoulder has grown to nearly the size of a grapefruit, a partially flattened one and one, of course, that is covered with fur. On her small frame, this lump is substantial. Pangs jab mercilessly at my heart; I cannot fathom, much less accept, the injustice of this invasion in the body, the physical home, of my healthy, agile, athletic pup.

They say that desperate times call for desperate measures. Also, when times are dire, you request "all hands on deck." This is, to be sure, a time of need – and so I have called upon everyone I could think of, including, at the suggestion of a psychic whom I'd consulted for myself, an animal healer. Always trying to make sense of my own life, my personal challenges and roadblocks and shortcomings, I've found intuitives to be tremendously helpful. They have given me useful guidance, helped me chart my journey and improve upon this work in progress which I call my self. For Zoey, I held out hope that a psychic who focuses on animals, an animal healer as it were, might be able to access something, some layer of understanding or information, hidden from the rest of us and which might, just might, give me clues as to what is going on, how I can help.

I dialed the recommended healer, Sallie, at the agreed-upon time, and she answered on the first ring. A minute or two of introductions sufficed, and she was ready for business. I, it turned out, was extraneous; my role consisted of hanging up, and then answering the phone when she called again forty-five minutes later. Okay, I can do this, I told myself, and hung up. It was a relief, in fact, to hand the reins over to another, someone with powers beyond my own.

While I talked to Sallie, Zoey had been lying curled in her usual position, her muzzle resting on her paws, all four of which were drawn together to form a cradle for her head. She had been quiet, sleeping. Moments after my talk with Sallie ended and I had been, for all practical purposes, dismissed, Zoey lifted her head. And then she began to vocalize. It was a strange sound, unlike anything she'd previously emitted, almost suggestive of a dog talking (if a dog *could* talk), a continuous up-and-down-and-around "roooo." Very, very odd. At some point, the roo'ing stopped and Zoey rested her head back again on her paws, as if nothing unusual had happened. Immediately, the phone rang. It was Sallie.

The reading began with an account of the history of the land on which we lived, the indigenous Americanv tribe who had lived nearby many generations ago, altercations between people at the site of our home that, over centuries, had instilled various energies in the area, as well as other influences (climate, geology) that have an impact on the animals living there today. It encompassed everything from Zoey's perceived role in the family (among them, she believes it is her job to help Carolyn express herself) to her food preferences and current nutritional needs, given her illness. Specific foods, including duck and sweet potato, were in order. How is she feeling now?, I wanted to know. During her time spent remotely with Zoey, Sallie had asked; she reported to me that Zoey's legs hurt. asked; she reported to me that Zoey's legs hurt. A pang shot through my heart, simultaneously sinking my spirits.

For Zoey and me, the experience of this cancer, the suffering it brings, is far different. Zoey is grappling with cancer's physical impact, the direct sensations and physiological results of having marauding troops storm through her body, attacking both the structures that support her and the functions that hold her life together. For me, on the other hand, the suffering has the qualities of sorrow and fear.

What does Zoey know of fear? She has led a charmed life, protected in every way, never once facing physical danger, unless of course we count the streets we cross every day. Thunder scares her, sends her squirming under my bed and cowering at the farthest corner, quivering when the booms are especially loud. But once the storm passes, her fear is gone, completely, and along with the fear itself goes all memory of it. What fear she does experience is almost more of a physical response than an emotional one, as there is no thought process attached, no rumination involved, and no retrospective review or future projection – the loci of so much of what we experience as emotion. You might argue that there is relatively little suffering in this immediate physical sort of fear; it is short-lived, acute but fleeting.

My fear, and human fear in general, staggers under the weight of the future. What will happen to this cancer? Will it damage her organs, causing all sorts of havoc? Will it create pain, and will that pain escalate, out of control, indefinitely? What if it can't be controlled, if it all becomes unmanageable? What will I do?? My fear has two sides: a fear *for,* a dread of what Zoey may endure in days to come; and powerlessness, the horror of not being able to help. I am afraid of what may be urgent, but beyond my capacities – to assuage, to comfort, to help.

With respect to physical prowess, small dogs fall into two categories – the lapdogs and the athletes. Lapdogs don't require, or even want, vigorous exercise. Athletic dogs crave it, glory in it, seek it out. Zoey, a mutt with undeniable terrier influence, falls into the latter camp. She adores her walks, but her true love is unleashed, uninhibited motion. She throws her whole body into her runs, twists, turns, dashes. My daughter and her friends call these fits of energy Zoey's "spasm," a bit of a misnomer but a code word (age-appropriate for the elementary schooler), nonetheless, for those times when Zoey tears about in a joyous frenzy, dashing alongside the creek or through the woods with kids in hot pursuit.

Though certain situations posing physical risk can cause her to hesitate – she balks, and then tiptoes across, a swinging footbridge along one of our hikes, for instance – Zoey has never questioned her own strength or balance. She will scramble up a boulder many times her size, jump onto a high ledge, and leap with abandon across a ditch. In her mind's eye, she is more powerful than a locomotive, and possibly even able to leap tall buildings in a single bound.

The only pup in a litter of three (the remaining two being Sam and Carolyn), Zoey matches her physical feats to those around her. Those counterparts are not canine.

When the kids were younger, jumping on the bed was a daily pastime. I actually encouraged this, and the game became something akin to a ritual. In those days, before our bank account could comfortably handle the expense of an actual bed, my ex-husband and I slept on a mattress on the floor. It was covered by our down comforter sporting an underwater scene in which whimsical, brightly colored, artfully stylized, tropical fish swam playfully around a coral reef. The game was called "which one shall I jump to?" and my role was to answer this question by pointing to one of the fish, perhaps a pink polka-dotted eel or a lime-green and canary-yellow angel fish. Depending on who was jumping, I might point to one of the fish in the middle of the scene or to the far edge for a special challenge. Then a small boy or girl, usually squealing with glee, would fling him or herself across the turquoise expanse and land, sprawled or in a heap, on the appointed spot.

When we upgraded to a bed, the game became more challenging, but then, too, the kids had grown bigger. Not so, Zoey. While the kids now had to jump vertically as well as horizontally, to reach a targeted fish or piece of coral, Zoey had to perform a superhuman feat. Without doubting herself, or even hesitating to assess the situation, she rose to the challenge. To this day, she launches herself, in a single bound, onto my lofty bed which, I should note, conjures up visions of the princess and the pea.

Perhaps because of her athleticism, throughout her life and despite a ravenous appetite for food of every sort, Zoey has maintained a svelte but strong physique. Today she is nine years old, and until recently, when her disease began to slow her pace and alter her shape, she was often mistaken for a puppy. Her prodigious cuteness, of course, contributed to this illusion. It's a peculiar warp in our culture, perhaps, but cuteness, even more than strength, signifies youth, and youth draws approval. People approach youth, they comment positively on cuteness and on strength. Contrast this with the typical response to the aged, under-confident, or infirm – the weak. Hmmm.

For the past five years, I have had my fine, stick straight, blond hair, limp as corn silk, cut by a man who knows about strength. The irony is probably lost on most of his clients, who revere him for his warmth and easy-going nature, as well as his excellence with difficult hair. Consistently ranked in the top ten in Southeastern regional body-building competitions, Willard is massive. His biceps, by his own description, are not guns but cantelopes. His numerous other distinct and well-defined (not to mention large) muscles fall in step, each toned and proportionate to its neighbors. There's no denying that, physically, Willard is strong.

Willard and I became friends based on easy humor and enjoyment of each other's company; we didn't have any classic or motion picture-like chemistry, didn't bond immediately over common background, or didn't share much in the way of interests. I do, however, love to exercise, and have always involved myself in a variety of activities that involve my body. In addition to matters related to fitness – spanning life, the universe, and everything – we shared notes on being single. I was a bit more of a veteran than Willard, being several years out from my divorce and having, shall we say, explored the options. For starters, I had tried the personal ads in the local independent press, and then in bolder days, I progressed to match.com, e-harmony, singles events, speed dating and, well, anything that I could think of. For Willard, these were impressive and daring moves, lying well beyond his capacities at the time.

One question encapsulates a perennial puzzle confronting the single woman, or perhaps any woman, and this question is "what do men want?" It catalyzes all manner of speculation, causes no end of confusion. I once asked Willard this question, specific to him: "What do you most look for in a woman?" Without hesitation came his one-word reply, "Strength." Despite his focus on physical strength, this time he did not mean musculature.

Willard possessed strength of character, at least in equal measure to his physical strength, and he knew it. Like many Black American males, he had spent ten good years, from age 16 to 26, in prison. He, himself, hadn't committed a crime. In the wrong place at the wrong time, he had been rounded up at the scene of a violent brawl along with numerous other young Black males in this country, condemned partly by proximity to the event, and largely by skin color. He emerged from that prolonged incarceration, a life-changing and personality-shaping experience, not damaged but annealed. He learned to know, respect, and value himself – and to do so not weakly or apologetically, but emphatically.

As he followed his passion (hair) and plotted his career, it must have taken strength to present himself as a man, a straight Black man, in a world populated by hair stylists, aestheticians, and beauticians. The assumptions, almost platitudinous, are made. But by dint of his strength, Willard managed to both dismiss and circumvent them. No one, it is safe to say absolutely no one, would question his manliness.

One of Willard's foibles was his out-and-out refusal to own a car; he chose to walk everywhere, to spend his substantial tips not on gas and automobile insurance but on international travel. This must have perplexed his family – a mother, brother, and "granny" – none of whom had ventured beyond a fifty-mile radius around their home, on the rural outskirts of Durham, North Carolina. Strength sometimes manifests as a willingness to be different, as an imperviousness to others' opinions and expectations, as an ability to listen to one's own desires and calling.

One winter evening, Willard asked me to drive him to a friend's house, so that he could pick up some music. From my home in Chapel Hill, this turned out to be a good half-hour drive, too far certainly for him to have walked and not falling on any public transit route. I owed him a favor in return for a haircut he had given me, off the salon books, so I willingly agreed. I showed up at the time he named, only to find that he wasn't quite ready. Waiting in the living room of his three-room apartment while he collected himself for the drive, I studied the collage of pictures plastering the thin walls. Some were photos; most had been clipped from an assortment of magazines, mostly featuring different hair styles or body-building competitors. A large full-color but scissor-cut picture, centrally placed, showed a nearly nude woman, in a few scanty pieces of faux leopard-skin, impaling herself (yes, her intimate female parts) on a spike.

Strength? I saw instead, now, the anger, over which strength had formed like a scab, a protective response guarding against a dangerous gush of emotion. Suddenly I'd had enough; I didn't want any connection to that underground reservoir of his past, and its aftermath.

With respect to anger, I have my own checkered past. While other children grew up haunted by the specter of monsters hiding in the closet, of demons out to get them or axe murderers under the bed, my fears were embodied in something more amorphous. Anger. The particular form it took was rage, on the part of my mother, directed at me. Throughout my early years and continuing into my adolescence, my mother yelled – not the so-called "yelling at me" that some kids complain of when they are chastised or criticized, but high volume, full-fury, vehement outbursts. She called it "blowing her top." In retrospect, I can imagine the frustration that fueled these attacks; my mother was a full-time, stay-at-home parent and housewife, saddled with four small children, before the era of disposable diapers (or even diaper service), and with a husband ensconced in a demanding career. To this day, she denies the extent of her anger, and the drama with which it erupted, claiming that children exaggerate their experiences. But would four children really fabricate the same memory? Would they all agree to be imprinted with these psychological footprints, and then to go through a decades-long charade of grappling with them?

The horror of anger, to a young child, is that it signifies an absence of love. Few things are more threatening, more frightening, at any age. And so, the repeated blasts of anger convinced me that my mother didn't love me; why else would she be angry with me so often, for so little? Simple logic. A child's logic, one-sided but explanatory.

Years later, married, I was shocked to watch deep springs of anger begin to bubble up from the depths of my husband's psyche. Like any idealist in the early stages of a relationship, and then as a fiancée and newlywed, I thought we were immune to anger, and most certainly to anger at each other. I believed that some things were mutually exclusive: we loved each other, therefore we could not be angry, or at least not angry for long, at one another. The fact that my bogey-man, the dreaded Anger, had found his way into my marriage hinted at nightmare.

As I see it now, unaware of my own unfinished business, of my unresolved relationship with anger, I inadvertently married someone who could give me another opportunity to work on this issue. I had failed Lesson #1, delivered to me at the feet of my mother. My strategy had been not to look anger in the face, but to run away from it, to seek an idyllic anger-free zone in which Love precluded Anger, not so much in defeating it as in totally transcending. I thought, in relationship, that I could find a haven, but Lesson #2 stood waiting for me, to be delivered by none other than my husband. Still, I resisted the lesson. I placated. I avoided. It took many years for me to recognize the dynamic at play, and more to examine it honestly. What is it telling me about myself? About my past, the wounds I need to heal? Can I meet anger in a way that presses my growth edges, rather than sending me into retreat? After all, it is the rocks that make for rapids. And not only do the rapids give us the thrill of movement and excitement, they also make the calm of flat water downstream ever so much sweeter, more peaceful, delightful.

At forty years old, one might suppose that I had finally taken on Anger, attempted to befriend it, and learned to stand up for myself when it misbehaved. That level of self-empowerment lay still a few more years ahead. Rather, it took the startling awareness that this anger, an unwelcome energy in the household, was harming my son, my precious innocent little boy, before I could deliver the final blow to our marriage. On some level, I must have believed that I, myself, deserved the two faces of this anger – resentment and coldness on the one hand, heat and drama on the other. But Sam, I knew for certain, did not deserve it. At his age, I had known the hurt of anger, and worse, the even deeper pain of what that emotion means to a child. So I asked my husband, the father of my children, to leave.

He said, "I'll need two weeks to find a place." That's all.

The post-divorce phase has been, for me, a long, strengthening journey. The path of life becomes clearer with each passing year, and the simplicity of it amazes me. Strength, I have learned, is not power; it is not demonstrated through heavy hitter emotions, like anger or even passion. It is quiet and unassuming. I think strength, true strength, is actually a very internal affair, and mostly a by-product of self-love. No wonder we meet so few people who possess genuine strength – loving one's self is perhaps the hardest, and the most universal, task, but it's one that we all are given.

How much easier it is to work on the showy kind of strength, the kind that manifests as physical prowess (marathon, anyone?), or in professional success, or popularity and social stature. But to work on loving ourselves? This is just plain hard. Hefty forces inhibit us: the fear of others' judgment, of being considered selfish, of no longer receiving because we are no longer needy. We resist the exposure, the nakedness, of recognizing ourselves as the legitimate source of the love in our lives. We want, desperately, for love to come from another, hopefully from a spouse or partner – but these others can only confirm what we already know about our inherent loveableness. They can provide us with an outlet for the love that spills over and streams through us, and they can mirror the love that is within us, but they cannot make us feel *loved*. Ironically, when we are loved, from within and by ourselves, we have no needs – for approval, things, people, accomplishments, circumstances. What greater strength than this?

8

Many dogs, Zoey among them, harbor a soft white tummy. The skin on Zoey's belly has a pinkish hue, speckled with a few dark splotches, and with only the barest covering of wispy fur. Naturally, the pattern of her belly is simply an extension of the patterned skin that covers her whole body, and in areas where her short glossy fur is white and sparse, her legs, for example, spots of darker skin show through. In her most casual family moments, her approximation of intimacy, Zoey rolls onto her back, legs relaxed but poised mid-air, and exposes her tummy for caressing. In these times, her energy is at its softest.

Mostly, of course, Zoey's belly is hidden from view. Other dogs don't sniff there; unfamiliar people don't reach down to pat her there; she, herself, can't see, smell, lick, or even scratch it.

Recently, for several months, I dated a man who had served twenty-five years in the United States Marine Corps. He had risen up the ranks of the Marines through sheer determination, fearlessness, and a sense of responsibility. His integrity was indisputable. Nick had traveled the globe, shot (humans) and been shot at, crawled on his belly through enemy fire in the middle of the night, survived for months in the arctic without heat or proper shelter. Fear simply had no role, not even a bit part, in his history.

In internet dating, a first "meeting" is actually more like a mutual interview. Having exchanged some basic information via email and phone (the cover letter and resume phase), you meet to see if you actually want to, well, *meet*. These first screenings are often just twenty minutes, usually involving coffee. My first date with Nick, however, was a walk. This may not have been the most romantic of introductions; it turns out to be a context not exactly conducive to flirting. I might reconsider the strategy in the future. But I've vowed never to even consider a man for his relationship potential if he's not a walker. There's too much pleasure in walking together, too much opportunity to share thoughts and feelings, too much time for souls to mingle – and conversely, the potential loss, in not walking together, is too great. Non-negotiable, this prerequisite. And so, Nick and I walked and he told me a story.

The training of a Marine begins in boot camp, where the physical tests range from the challenging to the near-impossible. The shadow of humiliation lurks behind each feat, should one fall short of expectation, and the line between expectation and requirement is thin. But Marines do struggle, and when they fail, they are not sheltered from shame. Marine Corps training lacks compassion for this version of suffering, inflicted at the hands of both superiors and peers, fellow men in identical circumstances.

On one of Nick's first days in the Marines, the superiors commanded his troop to race through an obstacle course. There were ropes and ditches and ladders associated with all manner of unlikely tasks. Nearing the end of this grueling line-up of physical challenges, Nick came to a concrete wall. It was ten feet high, solid, smooth and, to any normal person, insurmountable. Every rookie was to scale the wall, stand on its top, all of six inches wide, and then jump down on the other side. No exceptions. Nick ran at that wall, hurled himself at it, scrambled, grappled, and failed, falling back to the ground bruised in more ways than one. Again, he ran, leaped, struggled, and fell back, on the same side. Others passed him by, scaling and jumping off the top to continue the course, as he tried again, and again.

Now Nick is not exactly a tall man; I'd estimate five foot eight inches in his thickest soled shoes. Others, taller Marines, jumped or scaled the wall successfully on their first or second try, and proceeded onward to the next obstacle. Nick did, finally, make it over after numerous attempts, but with a sense of humbled self-assessment. Years later, a superior who had observed his unflagging efforts offered his perspective, and a backhanded affirmation, "Watching that performance, I knew you'd go far in the Marines. We look for people like you – the ones who don't give up." In fact, Nick retired after twenty-five years of service, a decorated lieutenant colonel.

In earlier years, I might have agreed with the Marine Corps approach. For years, I have been an iron-fisted taskmaster, setting goals and holding myself to them. It was a double standard of sorts, as I wasn't nearly so demanding of my kids, definitely not of my husband, or anyone else for that matter. This rigor applied, specifically, to me. My self-discipline, I'm sure, has looked like strength in the eyes of onlookers. Discipline and determination will get you over certain sorts of walls – academic ones, athletic ones, financial ones, even some types of social and interpersonal ones. But these traits constitute a muscling-through, Marines-style, of personal challenges. They cannot teach the strength entailed in vulnerability, in exposing the soft white underbelly.

Why are we drawn to the pearl, as an image of beauty, perfect in its imperfection? We could substitute something with a cleaner origin, say, a snowflake. Like a pearl, a snowflake also symbolizes purity; it flutters peacefully down on us from above, the heavenly realms. We marvel at them for their uniqueness, but not as paragons of beauty. Both pearls and snowflakes form around a core of dirt. But pearls grow in the deep and dark, in the humblest of settings, the dark irregular grey interior not of an especially beautiful seashell but of a rough and undistinguished mollusk; they take form in depths where they are enclosed, hidden.

Think, too, of the lotus, a flower revered in the East as a symbol of true inner beauty; it emerges from mud, all the more pure and white for its incongruous backdrop, its ability to rise through and above its surroundings, unscathed. We see potential, the promise of beauty, intrinsic in the rocky, the hard, the challenging. Isn't the image of a diamond in the rough more compelling than that of, simply, a diamond?

Is our beauty, our inner loveliness, given greater depth and appeal by its own muddy background, a unique history of pain, of lessons and challenges faced with courage or maybe with poignant and sincere weakness, of our acceptance or possibly our bravery in the face of our own limits?

My divorce heralded a phase of sheer endurance, in which blow after blow required me to recover, reestablish my stability, and then take another knock. Things in my house broke down like falling dominoes, one coming upon the heels of another. Friendships faltered. The universe seemed to be whittling away, systematically, at the elements that had made up my life, as I knew it.

A couple of truths emerged in this battering. For one, I learned that strength lies not as much in standing tall and holding one's own against a blow, but in the flexibility to take the blow, to fall down without falling apart, to adapt, reconfigure, and re-create at best, but when that is not possible, at least to carry on in the face of change. I also learned something about queuing, an antidote to the urgency that can overwhelm when multiple needs occur all at once. Certain things can wait; certain ones can be allowed to never happen; issues can be handled each in due time, sequentially. Here strength resides in having sufficient confidence to hold off, not to rush pell-mell on all fronts but to take one step at a time, knowing that all will, ultimately, be resolved.

My divorce created internal disarray as well, a mirror reflection of the external disintegration of my life. Gone was the vision, formed over my first twenty-five or so years, of my next fifty years. What did my life look like without a central love relationship? I had no idea what the contours of a vision to replace that one would be. And to be honest, being still committed to that ideal, I had no desire to forge a new concept. In the absence of an Other, a partner on life's path, I had no choice but to recognize my alone-ness. Reluctant, disappointed, I could only note that I didn't like the picture of living by, with, and for my self.

The intervening six years have led me through a labyrinth of self-discovery, way leading on to way (as Robert Frost would have it), toward a new and conscious relationship with my Self. It has much to do with accepting my own soft underbelly. I am a much stronger, self-possessed, and happy person now that I have learned to live with my vulnerabilities exposed, at least to myself, in intimate honesty, without apology or explanation. I have nothing to prove other than who I am, and that, it turns out, encompasses a kaleidoscope of feelings, strengths, weaknesses, goals and dreams, disappointments, hopes, fears and aspirations. I have muscle, yes, and also a soft underbelly.

$\mathcal{9}$

There's a certain rawness about pain. It cuts to the core, searing, drilling into the deepest, and the softest, parts of ourselves. I resent it. In general, I keep a positive attitude, look on the bright side, seek out the good and the beautiful in my life and surroundings – and I savor them, with gratitude. I am aware of the good fortune I've had, the many privileges and blessings that, for no particular reason, have come my way. I love my life. Against this backdrop, itself a choice, heartbreak is an unwelcome intrusion.

Zoey doesn't feel well today. She was sick overnight, and I had been oblivious to her misery. My alarm went off at the usual time, and in the dark, making my way across my bedroom to put a halt to the noxious bleeping, I stepped in the squishy evidence. My disgust was rivaled only by my distress at what this deposit on the carpet implied. Pup failed to rise with me; she needed me to carry her downstairs and outside for her "business," in the backyard where she might have some semblance of privacy. I continue to impute this sort of concern into the situation, though I know in my heart of hearts that Zoey's current degree of illness makes a concept like privacy pale, almost silly.

My hopes lifted slightly when she ate her lamb and rice dog food, a healing formula suggested by Sallie, the pet psychic, which I purchased by mail order at top dollar. Supposedly it will help boost her beleaguered immune system. She's taking vitamin C, a tablet encouragingly named "K-9 Immunity," and cod liver oil capsules, all smeared with organic peanut butter and drizzled with cold-pressed, extra virgin, olive oil. (So far, she seems quite satisfied with the dietary repercussions of her illness.) After eating, she placed herself carefully on a cushion, but didn't lay her head down, a sign of obvious discomfort. My heart sorrows for her.

A diagnosis of cancer, whether in a person or a pet, shatters the world as you know it. It is, in short, a personal cataclysm, sending shock waves through one's whole being, rendering daily routines at the same time meaningless and critically important, knocking everything once familiar off course.

Zoey was diagnosed on Martin Luther King, Jr. Day. Ever after, this holiday will carry for me the taint of association. But as I recognize this, I am also humbled to consider that no day, not a single one among the 365 options in the calendar, goes by without someone, somewhere, suffering a similar association. Any suffering, but especially the prolonged and anticipatory kind, may be an intensely personal experience, but simultaneously there is nothing at all personal about it. It is ubiquitous, common.

Shortly after receiving Zoey's diagnosis, I enacted my usual strategy for managing situations where I recognize I'm in over my head, namely, I talked to people, soliciting their advice, experiences, suggestions, knowledge. Out of this process, often, emerges wisdom – and so I hoped. I asked a good number of people about how they handled their dogs' cancers. Co-workers, neighbors, a sister, acquaintances – many people, it turns out, have lived through similar disasters with their pets. I plied them for advice about dealing with the cancer: Should I take Zoey to the veterinary oncologist? Consider chemotherapy? Seek out a second opinion or additional tests? Have the surgeon remove the obvious first lesions? Was it unrealistic to hope for remission? To me, the decisions were overwhelming, and my path totally unclear.

Yet I found, in the midst of my grief and in the throes of indecision, a comfort in camaraderie. Others had known this despair, had suffered this heartbreak. I look around me and wonder, how many have faced something akin to my despair? In the grocery store, on the street, at the library, I silently marvel – Did you? Or you?

My son, Sam, was born in October 1989, on the eve of the Loma Prieta earthquake, which badly shook San Francisco and much of the Bay Area were badly shaken. National news played and replayed a film clip of the Bay Bridge collapsing; one car perched precariously on the extreme edge as the portion just in front of it dropped into the water far below. The bridge looked flimsy, and the auto poised at the cusp of disaster, like a matchbox car. Meantime, on the other side of the bay, a freeway exchange in Oakland collapsed, killing a couple hundred people. And in San Francisco, homes and apartment buildings near the water, the low parts built upon landfill, crumbled. A day before, these various human creations, constructed of concrete and steel, had given the illusion of solidity, and then, a mere few seconds of tremor, the hand of the earth in motion, had shaken not only edifices but also assumptions – of what is secure, what is permanent, what we can count on.

A new mother as of only a few hours, I stood on the roof of Alta Bates Hospital in Berkeley, with my ex-husband who, in gym shorts and a tee- shirt, out-dressed me in a hospital gown (a glamorized term for a large, shapeless patch of cloth, nondescript in color, half-heartedly decorated with a miniscule fleur-de-lis pattern). It was early evening, and we looked out over the gradually darkening neighborhoods of Berkeley and Oakland. Smudges of smoke punctuated the eery unlit streets. At that point, the pain of this community, our community, was ungraspable, surreal. Our personal world had endured its own ground-shaking event, as transformational as the disaster around us, and the birth of our first child made it hard to comprehend another, parallel, universe of change – change on a much larger scale, affecting many more, but to us, comparable in significance.

Sam arrived more or less on time, deeply wanted and anticipated with joy. Determined to bring my baby into the world in the best possible way, I had prepared with natural childbirth classes. My ex-husband, though he didn't share my enthusiasm for things alternative and holistic, dutifully accompanied me. His role, primarily, was to learn the positions that ease the pain, and to intone "breathe, breathe," empathically, along with other obvious phrases. Given that this support and these utterances were not natural for him, we were both acquiring the skills of natural childbirth.

Despite ten weeks of preparation, we nonetheless arrived at the hospital totally unready for a rapid succession of events. The birthing process proceeded as expected for many hours, but at about Hour 13 took an alarming turn. My doctor became less chatty, more serious, and then adopted a take-charge attitude. *"Don't breathe!,"* she commanded (hey, wait a minute) and nurses wheeled me into the operating room for, we thought, an emergency Caesarian. I, and more to the point, Sam, narrowly escaped that maneuver; my baby boy emerged at the very last minute, umbilical cord wrapped around his neck, blue, barely measuring any vital signs, failing to emit that first, long-awaited wail. Surprisingly, for a few tense moments, my pain withdrew from my sphere of awareness, as if recognizing its place in priority behind the urgency of a baby's first breath.

The pain, as with all labor and delivery I'm sure, had started out fairly manageable. I was swimming my usual morning laps when the first contractions hit. Knowing I had many hours ahead, and a long slow crescendo, I kept swimming, pausing at the end of the lane when a contraction struck, mild in that early phase, then resuming again when it passed. Back home, I vacuumed the apartment (I hated the idea of returning to a mess); finished my thank-you notes for baby shower presents; and walked down the street to the mailbox to post them. Things were basically in order, my day begun as it should, before we headed to the hospital, driving at the speed limit, not above, and parking in the deck.

On entrance, I confidently informed the Obstetrics nurse that I didn't want anesthesia. I had, after all, planned for a natural childbirth; I was ready. Hours later, between double-you-over contractions, I begged for... not relaxing warm blankets and aromatherapy, but drugs. Strong ones, the heavy artillery. The pain started to press the bounds of what I could endure. "It's too late, honey," the nurse said sweetly, almost comfortingly. Fear set in. What would happen to me if I couldn't manage this pain? Already it was more than I could bear, coming in waves, unremittingly, certain to escalate. There was clearly no turning back, at this point, from a future that inspired abject horror. Competent assistants flitted in and out, some remaining positioned around me, but there was no one to help, no one who could get me through this unendurable pain.

How many thousands of women live through labor every hour of every day? Leaving the hospital with a healthy baby boy, I looked around me in awe. Women were everywhere, strong, tempered-by-fire, beings – mothers. I walked down the sidewalks of North Oakland wondering, you – did you live through it? How did *you* manage?? And you? And you? They looked so nonchalant, going about their daily lives as if nothing unusual had happened. How could they all, each one of these women, these mothers, have been so strong? A bond of admiration grew in me for them, so different from one another, so varying in their circumstances, their appearances, their characters, yet all so experienced. I felt myself a newcomer to this web of shared pain, endurance, survival, and amnesia – a community welded by the lesson, perhaps, that we are nothing special, and at the same time, that we are all amazing. That we can get through even the hardest of times, and on the other side of that tunnel we find nothing other than life, continuing with or without us, but continuing just the same.

For, out of this pain emerges love, the intense bond with tiny beings, our babies, for whom we endured so much. It is a platitude that a mother's love is a universal, unshakable, phenomenon, a basic instinct and truth. What is not so obvious, nor so well understood, is how this infinitely intimate experience, this pain that one faces utterly alone, this pain that marks both the beginning of a new life and a transformation of the life we once knew, alchemizes into something as general, as pervasive, as love.

We suffer extremes of pain at life's beginning and also at its end. Birth and death, the bookends of our physical existence, at least as we know it, are bounded this way. But pain is only one side of the coin. The joy that accompanies pain, when a birth ushers in new life, sustains us through the discomforts of pregnancy and the suffering of delivery; it is the true midwife, easing the transition inherent in birth.

What guides us, helps us, gives us hope, through our struggles with that other transition, death? Unlike with a birth, the path beyond a death remains hidden, its joy obscured. Perhaps the events of our lives have prepared us, by building within us the strength to trust in a future joy, without the need to see it, and without the security of a road map to get us there. Or perhaps we haven't developed this strength, haven't confronted and overcome a series of challenges, internalizing the lessons; then, we face death with fear and a sense of loss. In either case, if we can imagine joy hiding timidly behind pain, if we can discern both in the faces surrounding us and accept their companionship, we find a community of suffering. Despair is there, and sometimes, but not always, hope. This community, known or unknown, offers a blanket of compassion that can salve our aching core.

Pain, I am learning, does not damage love, nor eclipse it. No, in its heat it sears the raw and simple truth of love into the deepest folds of our being. Pain, in one sense and at great cost, immortalizes our love.

I remember the day I forgot how to play. I was thirteen years old; my younger sister, Mary, was ten. Despite my intense jealousy toward this smaller and undeniably cuter sibling, we had been playmates for the duration of our short lives – in the bathtub when we were teeny, then after school as we grew up and went not quite separate enough ways, and on family vacations that brought us all, four children close in age, back together, sometimes happily, other times too close for comfort. Our older sister and brother had better things to do than pass their time with the younger twosome, and so Mary and I made use of one another's company for that primary purpose of any child, play.

On this particular afternoon, a quintessential New England fall day, dry leaves swirled in a chilly wind, gusty and brisk. A heavily overcast sky loomed overhead, nearer for the weight of the dark gray clouds it contained. School was over for the day. Jam-packed yellow-orange buses had delivered us, me from junior high and my sister from elementary school, to the nearest street corner. Our route from the bus stop to home involved a short walk up a dead end street, an obstacle course of potholes from winter heaves, across a neighbor's yard, through a gap in a partially tumbled-down stone wall, vines working their way through and over it, and along a narrow footpath leading to our back door.

Typically, on these afternoons, with only a couple daylight hours remaining, we quickly downed a glass of milk and a couple homemade cookies (my mother's crisp oatmeal raisin cookies have become a family legend) and headed outdoors to play. At the time, our family lived in a house which my parents discretely dismissed as a "white elephant." The kids at school, a little more grandiosely, called it a mansion. Our yard, at least a full acre, matched the edifice in proportion and rundown grandeur. It comprised the remains of what must have been a lovely formal garden with ancient peonies and other exotic perennials, still thriving amid a tangle of weeds and nightshade, swathes of green grass shaded by tall and graceful black locust trees along either side of the driveway, a more casual backyard with lilacs that bloomed in numerous lush shades of purple, a now-overgrown rock garden to the far back, space behind a brick four-car garage for each of us children to have a garden plot, a woodsy side yard, and a small recessed space which seemed to have been set aside to serve as home to a giant red beech tree. From a limb of this tree hung a round wooden swing, dangling on a woven blue nylon rope, a birthday present given to Mary.

Mary and I headed for the swing. She jumped on it, abandoning any cares of the day in favor of its crazy twirling motion, its manic freedom. She spun around and around to get the rope tightly wound, then let loose, lifted her feet off the ground, spinning faster and faster as the cord unwound. Until now, I would have joined her in this realm of play, in this universe separate and apart from the world of school we'd just left behind. Time would have suspended its hold over me.

Today I felt different. Between yesterday and today, something inside me had shifted, as if I were a snake shedding a familiar skin and, with it, my lens on the world. With a cold clear-headed awareness, I sensed that I had moved on, I had woken up to a new reality which I had yet to accept. In this transition, somehow, in some way I couldn't define much less understand, the urge to play, to release myself to the child's world, had taken its leave. I couldn't slip into play mode, couldn't join her in the simple pleasure of the games we'd invent, couldn't let go of this new consciousness of self.

Aware that a major transition was in motion, what did I do? I faked it. We continued to play, and in doing so disingenuously, I developed a shameful sense of my own misfit, of a phoniness that I couldn't admit. And I mourned the loss – I had changed, unwittingly and not by choice, and the casualty had been my own ability to have fun.

I love to watch Zoey at play. Her favorite thing is to dash in hot pursuit, as if possessed. She releases her entire being into a chase; nothing else matters, or even exists, in her consciousness as she tears after a squealing child, or careens in circles after a canine playmate. On a trail, she often gets distracted by a scent or an obscure curiosity, a stump, say, or a heap of leaves; having fallen behind the rest of us, she races down the path to catch up, torpedo-like, her body compact and flying. "Gangway!" we shout in unison, bonded by this partly inside joke, partly family ritual.

At times, the urge to play comes over Zoey seemingly of its own accord. Gripped by an invisible force, a sudden need, she'll jump up, roust about the house until she finds a toy, trot victoriously back to one of her humans, toy in mouth, and entreat us to join the game. If we don't fall into step, grabbing it and pulling or taking off in the opposite direction, she'll toss it into the air with her own mouth, prance about, lower herself onto her front forearms with her rump in the air, wagging vigorously, glancing at us in the hopes that she can entice us into play.

Life as a single mom has its challenges, one of which is juggling the numerous tasks of work, house and home, and parenting, while maintaining some modicum of a life of one's own. A few years into this role, it dawned upon me that I was missing a major, and perhaps one of the more important, facets of life – play. I had managed to keep up with so many obligations and responsibilities, the "shoulds" of this phase of my life, largely focused on mundane tasks and others' needs. I routinely violated an 11th commandment I'd once seen on a poster in my college chaplain's office, "Thou shalt not should." In the effort to support a family on my own, I hadn't managed to retain fun in the first five, or even the top ten, aspects of my days. Then and there, I decided to weave play back into the fabric of my life.

Children, like dogs, play naturally. Spontaneously. They don't waste time deciding how they will play, what exactly they will do, when they will do it. They just simply play. I had, alas, lost this capacity long ago. To approach play now, at forty-something, I couldn't just slip into a spontaneous and free zone, that space where real play is possible, no, I had to do so consciously. The awareness of this difference mirrored the suddenly awakened feeling I'd had at thirteen. I had grown up.

Fortunately, Life gives us a second chance any time we opt for it, though this opportunity may not come in exactly the form that we envisioned, and usually doesn't replicate what we had the first time around. At this juncture, I decided, I could *choose* to play. I could define what would constitute fun for me, now, given who I am and at what point in my life. How to do this? When in doubt, I generally make a list. For straightforward things to be accomplished, this list might be very concrete – housework to be done, repairs to be prioritized, projects to be tackled. But for something creative, something to be imagined… this list needed to match, to be loose, open-ended, and able to evolve. And so I jotted down the parameters of play, *my own* play, my own *present-day* play: it should be colorful, messy, dynamic, textural, creative, free-form, and most importantly, devoid of any judgment or attachment to outcome.

That afternoon, in cut-off blue jean shorts and an old (dispensable) tee shirt, I sat down on my deck with four squeeze tubes of oil paint, the primary colors plus white, a heavy-duty paper plate that could stand in for a pallet, some extra-thick construction paper left over from the kids' school projects, a rectangular blue kitchen sponge, and a pair of scissors with which I cut the sponge into chunks I could hold between my fingers.

Conscious only of having fun, I lost myself entirely in the process of painting. Or was it merely the process of play? (Ask any amateur painter, and she or he will probably confirm the latter.) A longtime friend, over for a brief visit and viewing my latest painting project, summed up my process: "Now I see why you like this – it's like finger painting for grown-ups!" The pleasure of this experience, a gratifying immersion in timelessness, signaled to me that I was on the right track, hot on the trail not only of fun, but of contact with my soul. You might argue either that this process brings me deep within my self, or that it takes me transcendentally out of my self; ironically, the deep dive and the rise above seem to merge, to become one and the same. Speculations aside, the enjoyment that wells up in me as I play – in this case, with paint – tells me that I'm swimming in meaningful, too long neglected, waters.

I've since added fabric. I have a couple friends who, in different ways, create Things Of Beauty with fabric. One, a co-worker, sews impressive quilts. These, large enough to cover a queen-sized bed with a meticulous arrangement of tiny pieces of calico, are no small feat. She works from kits which contain pattern, instructions, and lists of "ingredients," that is, quantities of fabric, thread, specific needles and "foot" attachments for the sewing machine, sometimes embellishments such as velveteen trim or satin backing. Sitting at her sewing machine, over the course of several weeks, she stitches together pieces of cloth, measured and cut with precision, to construct heirlooms.

Another friend revels in color and exotic fabrics. She carefully designs tapestries, composed of exactly sized, precisely sewn, pieces joined into exquisite hangings. Her seams are flawless, all of her productions bear a professional touch. Still another friend, a co-worker, designs her own clothing, creating first the concept, then the pattern, and then the final product through rich textures and innovative combinations. They fit her elegantly, creating a polished and unique look, a verve, a style. These women create art. I am humbled.

My works, instead, are purely play. I stitch by hand, needle and thread moving in and out irregularly, leaving uneven edges and differently sized stitches. Because I don't bother to iron the seams, my pieces don't hang flat. I don't even plan my creations in advance, though I have a sense of the direction I want them to take. Rarely do I cut more than one or two pieces ahead of myself, rather, I snip out the next piece as I go along, however it strikes me at the moment. This color next? This fabric next to that one? I layer up swatches one piece at a time, letting the fabric guide me. There is no timeline to this play. Since I don't have a lot of time to devote, I return over the course of several months to the same project which, allowed this leisurely amount of time, evolves of its own volition. Divorced from outcome, I am along for the ride, enjoying the process.

I think I've learned how to play. Or, at least, I've found one way, among the millions of possibilities, to allow my soul to have fun – to immerse itself in purely unencumbered, unjudged, irrelevant, reckless, enjoyment. Lacking purpose but present to process, I play.

11

Zoey used to sleep in on weekend mornings. At some point when she was ready, she would rouse herself from her slumber, most likely with a good stretch, and bound down the beige carpeted stairs. Her whole body announced, with unabashed enthusiasm, "I'm up!!" This was no humble entry onto the scene, where I might be reading a book to the kids, or making breakfast; she made no semblance of qualifiers, no canine equivalent of apologies for bed-head hair or dark circles under her eyes. No, she burst forward with the exuberant news, complete in itself, that she is present in the world, today.

She has no history. Every day, whether she's coaxed out from under Carolyn's covers before dawn on a weekday, or rushes downstairs "late" in the morning (say, 7:00 a.m.) on a weekend, she starts fresh, unencumbered by her past. Devoid of retrospect, her freedom to begin anew is immense.

Throughout her life, Zoey has also managed to escape self-critique. She makes no excuses for her appearance. About a year ago, she began to go gray around the muzzle. This presented, to me, a puzzling phenomenon; in my eyes, Zoey had barely cleared puppy-hood. We still referred to her as "Pup," still spoke to her often in those higher register, babbling brook, tones universally reserved for the very young and the cute. Yet there they were, undeniably, white hairs sprinkled through the otherwise jet black portions of her face. There must be some mistake.

Other signs of aging have begun to creep in. She has warts, yes, and these do crop up in dogs as a sign of aging. People who sprout skin tags like to have them removed. Zoey couldn't have cared less, though my kids pushed for their excision. Bolstered by the vet's confidence that they were benign, I deferred to Zoey's inferred preference.

It is, perhaps, an indication of higher evolution that dogs don't concern themselves with aging, or with appearances in general. We human women should take notice – we may have a lot to learn. Today, for example, the majority of people who regularly have their faces injected with Botox are women in their mid-thirties; women's magazines purportedly targeted to women of all ages feature only models in their teens and early twenties, assiduously excluding the elderly (those over age thirty); a baffling array of products and cosmeceuticals (ponder on this word a moment – crazy!) offer to diminish our wrinkles (unsightly) or tighten our tissues (sagging). The images of beauty held up to us, in movies, magazines, television, basically all media, all look alike; they are all a bit too perfect, and always younger and more beautiful than us. Nonetheless, dutifully, we compare ourselves to these interchangeable other females, often in scathing detail. In so doing, we water the seeds of dissatisfaction – not a meaningful, productive dissatisfaction that calls us to a higher purpose or a better way of being, but dissatisfaction with our selves as defined by appearance, superficial transient appearance.

Zoey's gradual transformation is, if anything, not repulsive but endearing. Old dogs carry a dignity that borders on the poignant. They age innocently, un-self-consciously, and with unquestioning acceptance. We humans, by contrast, fight this natural process at every step. We do, however, have the option of practicing a measure of acceptance along the way – an acceptance not of choice, true, but as a bowing to inevitability, which marches hand in hand with perspective.

Today, in my mid-forties, I worry less about wrinkles than I did in my thirties. I have more, and they are deeper, but I focus on them less. This achievement is not to be under-estimated. My mother, my sisters, and I, not to mention uncles and cousins, are cursed with what my aunt who married into the family (thus spared) has termed "Maxwell skin." For the seeker of a firm complexion, it is the kiss of death, the dreaded end to our youthful beauty. Against the force of the Maxwell skin, moving as surely and as mercilessly as day turning to night, even the most potent overpriced face cream and spa treatments are powerless. Acceptance is the only option for the afflicted; the only choice is to recognize the personal challenge and work on the lesson.

I have noticed the same paradoxical shift – of advancing age leading to less, rather than more, concern for aging, and for appearance more generally – with a host of other personal complaints. The history of my life, from age six to age forty, can be traced as a string of consecutive, sometimes overlapping, self-castigations. Though they addressed most facets of my existence, many of these harsh self-directed criticisms were linked to physical embarrassments. Shapeless skinny legs, arms sporting too many blond hairs, pimples, limp and droopy hair, and the crowning blow, emerging late in the trajectory, wrinkles.

My fortieth birthday fell in the same year as the new millenium. It was a brave new frontier, a time of huge opening, for me – beginning, on January 1, 2000, with my bold move to ask my husband to leave. This was a totally unprecedented act of self-affirmation, absolutely the bravest thing I had done to date. (And there are other candidates for this designation, for example, as a thin, blond, twenty-year-old American, and female to boot, I hitchhiked alone through the Arava portion of the Negev Desert, in Israel – not smart, but possibly brave.)

Another, almost as daring, step was my decision, in that same year, to celebrate my own birthday. Emphasis here is on the concept, *my own*. I justified this to myself:

This was number forty, a big one. And it was my year to Acknowledge My Self, the year 2000, the year I stepped out of a bad marriage into the next chapter of my life.

The concept of celebrating myself, my own birthday, was alien terrain for me, and immensely daunting. As a child, with my August birthday falling during summer vacation, I hadn't had birthday parties; I jealously, but secretly, wished for those events to which I could invite my friends, with party games, crepe paper streamers, balloons, and all the joyous hullabaloo that goes along with a children's celebration. Instead, for a summer birthday, we had "family parties," subdued affairs with a standard menu, always the identical Betty Crocker angel food cake (no frosting), always the full family around the table, presents after dinner, expedient wrap-up so as to move on with the usual bedtime. Early in my marriage, my husband had been masterful at producing a good birthday, with surprises (oh joy!) and decorations, but that phase was history. In a divorce, or at least in my divorce, such memories of happiness died and were buried with the marriage.

Apparently now, at age forty and on my own, I had a choice: to have a birthday, or not to have a birthday, that was the question. It was up to me. Not parents, husband, or even friends, but me. The no-birthday option was definitely simpler, and more comfortable; after all, it offered me a golden opportunity to feel sorry for myself, to wallow in my circumstances, to confirm my unloveableness. It's always tempting to confirm what you already believe, especially about yourself. But, deep inside me, I was also nurturing a part of my self, a new and tentative part, that could stand up and say, "I'm here!," that could ask for what it wanted.

I chose the birthday option, and with it, the formidable tasks of swallowing my bashfulness, over-riding my sense of unworthiness, ignoring the inhibiting self-conscious voice within me, and taking this one on, all by myself. In character, my naturally unconventional character, it wouldn't be an ordinary party. It would involve a minimum of sitting around and chit-chat, which I am not very good at; instead, it would be centered around a hike in the verdant mid-summer North Carolina woods, along a trail beside the Eno River in Durham. This, by contrast, is something I'm quite good at. In lieu of presents, I asked the dozen or so friends I invited to bring gifts of themselves: the title of their favorite book, a favorite joke, and a favorite recipe. Everyone also brought an exotic fruit of their choosing, and together, we concocted a gigantic birthday fruit salad. Still somewhat the iconoclast and a long-time non-traditionalist, I dispensed with the usual trappings of birthday parties, including the cake. No thank you. One showed up, though, a yellow homemade layer cake with chocolate frosting (about as classic as could be), complete with a near-galaxy of tiny candles. Wine, too, appeared out of nowhere. It was, I'd say, a terrific launch for the next chapter of my life, a decade plus of single parenting.

Step by step, through that year and beyond, I began the difficult process of learning to value my self. Emily Dickinson is purported to have said, "As I age, my beauty steals inward." These are comforting words indeed. And it is true, as I ever-so-slowly uncover what might be beauty within, a beauty of the soul, of who I am, my wrinkles ever-so-gradually recede from view, becoming increasingly peripheral to my vision of my self. I don't doubt that others still see them, but now I don't care – at least, to be honest, I care less, and even less over time. Nor do I care whether others agree with what I'm finding as I explore my inner terrain, a landscape of hope and joy and love. I am coming to know it, myself; that will suffice.

I wonder if I'm approaching the freedom of a dog, that ability to live without concern for the opinions that others may hold of me, without fear of change in my physical form, without apology for what is.

12

If they could speak, mutts would have a lot to say about the way our human culture defines us. Mutts come in a vast variety of forms, of shape and size and color and texture of fur, of personality and behaviors. Diversity is their norm, and neither they, nor we, try to narrow the spectrum. But turning to ourselves, among humans, we take an altogether different approach; we make conformity the norm, holding ourselves and others to ideals – success, intelligence, beauty – that are decidedly monolithic. These are trumpeted in our media, through the news stories in business and politics, and in the pages of glamour magazines – which now target both women and men.

Zoey has the good taste not to spurn these prescriptions for how we should be, what we should aspire to, how we should measure ourselves; that would imply that they affect her in some way. No, she simply ignores them, like royalty not deigning to attend to influences well below her. Our standards of uniformity, promulgated through bastions of our culture, never enter her sphere of awareness, and I think she's a happier dog for the omission.

Many people have tried to grant Zoey status in a particular breed, as though simultaneously dignifying her and indicating a certain understanding on their own part. We often meet people along the bike path, or on a sidewalk, who offer a friendly guess at her lineage, usually choosing Jack Russell Terrier, close but to my mind not nearly as cute. When the film, The 101 Dalmations, made it big in all the major cinemas, not to mention as the packaging and toy prize theme in McDonald's Happy Meals, little children often squealed "Dalmation!!" with tremendous excitement, victorious in having identified a real-life example. And if a true Dalmation were shrunk proportionately, our 25-pound pup might, almost, have qualified for the distinction. The woman who owned Zoey's mother had claimed that she was a mix of fox terrier and Sheltie, though I defy anyone to find a hint of Sheltie in our Zoey. More honestly, she takes after her scrawny short-furred mother, which makes her the daughter of a decided mutt.

There's a certain charm in the uniqueness of mutts. Zoey, for instance, has large black splotches on her white fur, black speckles on her skin underlying the white, one ear that is jet black while the other is mottled white and black, a pink bald patch above her wet black nose, which turns a deeper pink in the summer from sunburn. She is adorable, original, unmatched.

I work in a professional context that honors appearances, blatantly values a woman's looks. Development officers at a distinguished university, typically, are some of the most fashionably dressed and most well-heeled individuals in the institution. They do, after all, present the face of the university to the world of the highbrow, the affluent. My female co-workers are practiced with make-up, masterful with accessories, polished in their personal presentation. Arriving recently and rather accidentally in this scene, well beyond my twenties and past, even, my thirties, I am behind in this domain. I figure that I lack the operative genes. On the few occasions when I attempt to apply make-up, I prove myself to be a bungling novice. I don't wear suits well; the fabric sits too stiffly on my body, as if aware of its place in my order of preference. My hair, quickly toweled dry in a locker room after my morning lap swim, doesn't arrange itself into any glamorous sort of coif, nor do I bother with blow dryer and mousse to help it. My shoes, well, these probably sum it up. While my co-workers wear fashionable shoes that taper to a feminine point as they approach the toe, the heel perched perilously atop a three- or four-inch spike, my shoes are rounded, low, New Age-y, and clunky by comparison. They have a comfortable look, as if they intend to befriend, to partner with, not to glamorize or reform, my feet. The feeling is mutual; I like my shoes.

I recently heard a perplexing, apparently philosophical, saying: "A woman's joy is her beauty." Hmmm, I thought, this could be taken two, diametrically opposed ways. On the not-so-encouraging side, it could mean that a woman derives her joy from her beauty. Uh oh. For those of us not so endowed, does this imply something falling short of joy? Or, alternatively, the intention could be that joy, an inner quality, is our true beauty – that our beauty actually does not lie in the usual outer measures of face, hair, physique, and the like. This kind of beauty radiates from within, regardless of those externals, stripping them of their import, outshining them as something we recognize to be inherently more precious.

I do make an effort to dress professionally; this is the reality of the workplace, and also carries undeniable impact on one's self-esteem. It does feel good to look "put together," as my mother would term it. (Think, for a moment, about how we express our emotional state in clothing terms: on the other end of the spectrum from being put together, we "come undone at the seams," or worse, "unraveled.") But I have ceased to compare my wardrobe to that of the others. My clothing is fine, despite the fact that I've acquired most of it from the thrift shop. Fortunately, wearing a size four and living in a community with a sizeable wealthy contingent, I can buy designer items at consignment with price tags in the single digits. I know that, more important than my look is the fact that my work is of high quality. I also know that my beauty lies beyond the realm of appearance, or even of competence. It rests, instead, somewhere in the balance of my enthusiasm, my love, and my happiness. Much as Zoey is most irresistible when immersed in play, or when ecstatically alive on a hike, or when delighted to see us return from an errand, I express my own radiance when I live in, and emanate, my joy.

Joy is unique to each person. Like a kaleidoscope, the quality of its radiance reflects our infinitude of facets and ever-changing inner experience. For on the inside, on the interior topography which encompasses our joys and sorrows and all other emotions, we are every bit as diverse as are mutts in their appearance. It follows that beauty, which we may believe to be determined by attributes and appearances, has little to do with those externals and everything to do with our inner, utterly individual, nature – specifically, our fount of fulfillment, our joy. When this shines through, we are all mutts, and we are all adorable.

13

Zoey's cancer is molding time, like taffy, in paradoxical ways, on the one hand stretching it out so that the minutia of physical change become apparent in excruciating detail, on the other hand compressing it so that the whole trajectory of her disease is happening just plain too fast, like a video player stuck on fast forward, not responding to my frantic attempts to play the film at a normal speed. A liveable and humane speed, one that allows time to acclimate, to process the information, to prepare. I am caught in the middle, a vise of past and future warped by pell-mell events, as if paralyzed by a sense of inevitability. Beyond going through the daily motions, beyond the effort of caring and caring for, what can I do? Worry.

I find myself worrying about Zoey's future a good bit these days. The hard lump on her shoulder has grown so that it sits, like armor, over her upper leg, extending on one axis from the base of her neck to her ribcage, and along the other, from the top of her leg to nearly her spine. On Zoey's petite but athletic physique, it is massive. Her morning walk today clearly challenged her. Whereas she used to relish this start-of-the-day ritual, our circuit around the block, sniffing intently at stops made by other dogs in the neighborhood, trotting dutifully along behind me, surging ahead when a cat appeared, phantom-like, in front of us, on this morning she grudgingly plodded along, without enthusiasm. I worry that her leg hurts.

In our daily ritual, the way that things *should* be, Zoey eats as soon as we get back to the house after her morning walk. We enter through the garage, take off our shoes (those of us who wear them), remove our leash (one of us), and hang up any jackets or outerwear, then immediately head for the food bowl. On an ordinary day, as it *should* be, Zoey is already ready and waiting at her bowl by the time I have untied, unzipped, and removed excess items, have walked the several paces from laundry room (which doubles as coat closet) to kitchen.

An onlooker might track the progression of Zoey's cancer by the contents of her food bowl. She now consumes a "healing formula" of inordinately expensive kibbles; following the orders of her animal healer, she has transitioned from a lamb and brown rice combination to kibbles featuring sweet potato and duck as principal ingredients. With this, she downs her supplements, as discussed: cod liver oil, K-9 Immunity, and recently added, Essiac Tea, in the original Canadian preparation hailed as an elixir for human cancer patients. She gets a couple tablespoons of whole milk (raw unpasteurized, the healthiest sort, teaming with probiotic immune-supportive bacteria) to help her swallow the Essiac. Foods resembling People Food have always held great appeal to Zoey, and she has relished her peanut butter-smeared pills as well as this interesting liquid combination, white and brown mixed into a sort of thick tan goo. This morning, Zoey settled on her cushion as soon as we returned from her walk, handling her body as though it suddenly weighed ten times its usual mass. No eager rush to the kitchen, no surge of energy and tail wagging in anticipation, no waiting patiently but happily for me to prepare her meal, pleasantly enhanced. Instead, I served her on her cushion, coaxing her to take nourishment.

My heart aches to see my pup unwell. This sorrow—a by-product of forethought, the ability, or more honestly the reflexive tendency, to think ahead— is the curse of being human. Despite my commitment to living in "the Now," to enjoying her presence, to being thankful for her life, each day that I still have Zoey, my mind races ahead to her future. Will she be sick for a long time? Is there any way to prevent her from suffering? What will happen to this awful lump? Will it spread to other parts of her body? How much bigger can it get?! How will I, and my kids, get through the progression of this disease? In short, I worry.

Worry is a human activity with, as far as I can discern, no correlate in the dog's psyche. To be sure, Zoey has nervous energy at times. She soothes herself by chewing on her paw; her mind stays out of the fray. This freedom from mental stress leads the dog owner to wonder… how have all our years of worrying actually served us? Have these volumes of worry helped us at all? It's doubtful that we can identify any accomplishments, satisfactions, or positive elements in our life that came to fruition because we worried.

A dog's response to potentially stressful situations is not to mull, but to act. Zoey can be calmly asleep on a pillow, peaceful and content. A noise our house catches her attention. Does she worry about who or what it might be? Does she roll forward in her mind to any number of possibilities and "what ifs"? Not at all. She jumps to action, her relaxed form suddenly charged with energy; she races to the door, exploding with shrill barks. My kids and I find this annoying. If I'm on the telephone, it's downright disruptive. I've sometimes thought it would be nice to have an easy-going dog, one who casually saunters to the door, tail wagging, or perhaps one who is hard of hearing.

Maybe, though, Zoey has a point. The threat of crisis – say, the appearance of an invader, a burglar, a suspicious person or dog – arises and, unencumbered by marginally helpful thoughts, she instantly moves to address it. Her body engages to the fullest, probably down to the cellular level and possibly to an even finer-toothed level of repercussions, to a cascade of neuropeptides. This instant alert leaves no room for mental gyrations or deliberation. She implicitly trusts her instincts, those mysterious responses residing in her body, rather than her lovely sloping cranium, to know the right thing to do. Once she acts, she is done, her work complete, and her mind free from the qualms of retrospect.

I, on the other hand, like to have evidence before choosing my actions. When major decisions stand before me, I look for a road map, borrow someone else's, or gather facts that will allow me to plan. Safely, in the broadest sense of that concept. Why do I *not* spring to action, moving forward confidently on the guidance of my instincts? In many situations, this would clearly be the more effective strategy, and would spare me considerable time and mental energy. The missing prerequisite for straightforward action, and possibly too a necessary precondition for spontaneity, is trust. The higher the stakes of the decision, the greater the need for trust – and ironically, the harder it is to come by.

In my thirteenth year of marriage, I was at wit's end. I had married young, for me. At age twenty-six, I had amassed a bachelor's degree from one Ivy League university and a master's from another. Like a collector of experiences, I had traveled for months on end, and had numerous adventures under my belt. But, largely due to my own lack of self-confidence and to the low value I placed on my self, I had minimal experience with relationships. I hadn't explored who I was through the mirror of an intimate other; I didn't even know what that sort of intimacy would look like – much less, how to create and nurture it, or how it would feel. Though, in my mind, I thought I had undergone extensive self-inquiry, through meditation and yoga and therapy and spiritual pursuits, I had done so in a vacuum. I didn't yet know my own soul.

Sentimental to the core, I had, since childhood, harbored visions of togetherness. I longed for a close warm relationship to anchor my life, a love-centered life. Unfortunately, being somewhat of a social misfit, I hadn't experimented with starter relationships in high school, those three- and four-week associations accompanied by adolescent drama. And in college, I hadn't allowed myself to truly enter any of the relationships that might have evolved (had I possessed a modicum of self-esteem); rather than daring to explore full openness and vulnerability, I had held back. Held what back? This I didn't even know.

Fear of judgment lurked always in the dim recesses of my awareness, never quite named but always there to steer me back into my private world. With the expectation of critique, I protected my self, guarding my inner terrain. This cautiousness, by the way, didn't jibe with my independent free-thinking exterior, the face I showed to the world. I was a walking study in cognitive (or personality) dissonance.

I married out of love, but also out of fear – fear that I would never find someone who could love me, fear of going through life alone, fear that I wasn't worthy of love, a secret I hoped would never come to light. Like many people, I suppose, I was aware of these sentiments, indulged in them sometimes, but I remained largely unconscious of the backdrop of fear that settled, like a bank of fog, between me and the life I might lead. It's not surprising that I made an unwise choice in marriage, as in many other things. For ironically, the universe delivers to us not what we envision but what we project. The fear I unwittingly harbored, that likely emanated from me at some level, trumped the true love I sought. And thus, what came to me was not an ideal partner, but one ideally competent and willing to confirm my dismal opinion of myself.

Fortunately, growing up is something we can do at any and all times of our lives. Through my thirties and forties, I consciously and diligently learned about life, self, and soul – usually backing into epiphanies through spiritual readings, yoga, and encounters with others who showed up at opportune times. I had no overarching strategy, no map that guided me in this process of personal growth, but I persisted nonetheless, goaded along by the concept that I, like everyone, was on a life journey to become a better, kinder, more loving and peaceful person. I worked on myself, systematically and with determination.

And so, after thirteen years of a marriage in which I felt fundamentally devalued, I arrived at a point, a pinnacle for me, where I could say, "I don't deserve this." Even beyond that, "I deserve better." Breakthrough! As the millennium approached and the darkness of November and December 1999 deepened, I lost sleep. Night after night, in the aftermath of this ground-shaking awakening, I lay in bed worrying about what to do. Divorce, a scary prospect, seemed dangerously close, but still taboo. I come, after all, from a family where the "D" word was something mentioned with sad faces, shaking of heads, the aura of collapse, disintegration, failure. It lay outside the realm of the possible.

My parents met in their twenties, my mother, the daughter of old-time Yankee stock, and my father, the older son of a farmer-turned-educator from rural eastern Kentucky. Their history prior to marriage was ridiculously brief: They had been once on a double date, though there had been no follow-through. Then, in a fateful moment, they bumped into each other in a ski lodge, one renting skis and the other replacing a broken pole. There was immediate attraction, a knowing on both sides, and, well… the rest, as they say, is history. A long history, of supposedly continuous harmony, a clear blue sky, a glassy lake without waves or ripples. They have passed their fiftieth anniversary, still inseparable. This picture, a model of successful marriage, I absorbed as unwittingly as a sponge. It shaped my expectations for my own Future. I never questioned Future. I never questioned that I would stay with my husband through thick and thin, no matter how tough the going became – but then, I never imagined what the "thick" might actually entail, how it might *feel*.

As our marriage teetered on an emotional precipice, poised to crash and shatter, there was also the issue of children, the internalized prohibition on breaking up a family, and the worry over what it would mean for their world, growth, development, and understanding of love and relationship. These things loomed larger than large; they were overwhelming. And so, night after night, at midnight and 1:00 and 2:00 a.m., I found myself grappling not with the big issues but with the mundane, easier to fret about, aspects of a divorced future – household budget, schedule scenarios, and the like. The path totally unclear, the roadmap absent, I was confronted with a situation in which I had no idea what was the "right" decision.

And then, inexplicably, one night clarity just happened, like a curtain lifting in my mind. I emerged from a state of dismayed paralysis to one of knowing that everything would be all right, that I *could* manage. With this trust came an immense sense of peace.

On New Year's Day, I asked my husband to move out of the house. The life-changing conversation was over in five minutes, and devoid of drama after all my anticipations of cataclysm.

Initially, post-separation, I worried about money considerably. I carried a pocket-sized memo notebook, and wrote down every penny I spent. I scrimped and saved. I cancelled all unnecessary expenses – cable TV, eating out, housecleaning, haircuts. I used generic shampoo, the local store's brand, unadorned and low on the chic index. Conditioner? Not needed. Miraculously, living in scarcity mode, we survived. With frugal measures in places, bills were paid, mouths were fed, and daily life went on.

Single parenting brought time challenges as well. I have friends who complain about the burden, the time constraints and time scarcity, when their husbands go away on business for a few days; they are stranded, left holding down the fort single-handedly. I attempt to be sympathetic, though my situation, the same situation, is permanent, save for alternate weekends of "visitation" (an odd term) stipulated by our divorce contract. Now having to support a family in more ways than one, I found myself burdened by the consciousness that the family's everything – financial, emotional, social, physical – depended on me. I made a silent and unshakable commitment to be the bedrock of my children's lives, regardless of what it would cost me personally.

As if healing a wound, allowing scar tissue to form and then the scar to fade from deep purple to faint blue-gray, time eased the open red rawness of being alone. Even a modus operandi as alien and threatening as single parenting, it seems, can become the new normal. And as I developed confidence that I could support my family, the worrying also abated. At some point, I don't remember exactly when, I abandoned the memo book in which I recorded each and every expense. Like a child outgrowing a well-worn and once indispensable stuffed animal, I reached for it less and less, and then not at all.

I began, tentatively, to buy a treat now and then. Frozen yogurt, mostly, and under a shadow of guilt, the guilt of the unworthy, of the self-indulgent (a designation which my mother had trained me to equate with inferior, as a human being). For a few months, I even hired a friendly, hard-working, young Hispanic woman, also financially strapped, to clean the house every two weeks, until she moved out of state to escape her abusive young husband. I allowed myself to order the occasional book, provided that I couldn't get it at our library, and that I was likely to hang onto, refer back to, and value it for the long term. Usually self-help or spirituality. I refinanced the house – in my own name. From the realm of fear, and despite a general not-knowing still pervading most aspects of my life, I had begun to acclimate, to find my bearings, and to dare to venture forth.

With Zoey's illness, I once again entered into a territory of utter and complete not knowing. What was the right course of action? My vet advocated strongly for specialized veterinary oncology. Under this option, I could take Zoey for a consultation, learn about the options – chemotherapy, radiation, surgery, and what each would entail – and I could choose to subject her to the recommended course of treatment. The cost, of course, would be astronomical. The prognosis, for a dog with a mast cell tumor growing at this pace, was not good, even if she were to receive aggressive medical treatment. Still, it might prolong her life… Or I could pursue alternative methods or care, none of which come with any guarantees. After anguishing over the decision, I opted for the latter.

In place of chemo, Zoey receives energy healing sessions at a distance. I have tremendous gratitude for our pet healer, working remotely from Nashville, and I trust in her efforts. But there are no guarantees, fewer even than the illusion provided by mainstream veterinary medicine, and there is no roadmap for her progression or her care.

I once phoned a well-known Buddhist author, a man currently living in Australia who had been one of the first Americans to receive the venerable designation of rishi. For me, the phone call constituted an impressive act of courage, made possible partly through a roundabout work connection, and partly by the fact that I was not doing this entirely on my own behalf. At the time, and to understate the situation, my son was struggling through adolescence – this was my legitimating context for talking to someone with Wisdom. And as a sidebar, I could use some insights into how to approach my own future, too.

In full disclosure, I had already consulted a soul reader in Portland, a woman named Marianne, who informed me that I possess strong intuitive gifts hidden, primarily, by self-doubt. Her message was emphatic, more like an admonishment than a neutral observation: I needed to access, release, and harness these inner capacities. Now, I've long been fascinated by the metaphysical, and I've wished that I, like the world's intuitives, could travel in the spiritual realms. But I couldn't. I viewed myself as a person fully stuck in the here and now, without a clue as to how to "read" more subtle realities, as one for whom the windows into psychic guidance and intuition remained firmly shuttered. Marianne's assessment therefore caught me off guard; I listened with hopeful interest, but reflexive skepticism. This did not jibe with the me I know. But then again, I am not one to ignore what I'm told to do; when someone says jump, I jump. What was my next step? Seek more evidence.

Two other psychics concurred with Marianne, to an eerie extent, duplicating not only her sizing up of my capacities, but her strong suggestions for how, in what areas, to work on myself. One of these readers urged me to go ahead, dispense with the extraneous things I was involved in (my job, for example), and begin my *real* life's work, that is, develop my psychic skills. "You should be doing what I am," he said. ("Hah!" responded my rational mind, aware of its own brick wall-like density.) I was at a loss. It was at this confused juncture that I called the Buddhist teacher, a person who had written prolifically on how to shine light into the deep interstices of the soul. After apologizing for the intrusion and requesting permission, I described my situation, and asked for his advice on how I could open myself to the unseen, the other side, when my starting point was a position of complete and total opacity. His words, spoken across continents, over thousands of miles including the entirety of the Pacific Ocean, emblazoned themselves in my mind as if delivered from three feet away. "The real issue is," he said, pausing briefly but meaningfully, "how comfortable can you be with the not knowing?"

Trust, as dogs seem to understand, is just that — a comfort in the face of not knowing, and an ability to proceed, to carry on with the basics of living, in the midst of it. For most of our lives, at least the juiciest or the most important parts, we don't have a roadmap. What we do have to go by, if we choose it, is the trust that we can manage, that we'll come through the deep and dark valley, the dense layer of cold damp mist, and will emerge on the other side, better for the journey, that we'll learn and grow despite – or maybe because of – what life throws at us. Trust is not about the particulars, it is not about having assurance of our ability to control those details that can be known; it is about the confidence, the deep-seated surety, that all is well, and that all will be well – given that we never, really, do know.

14

Desire is a much vilified emotion. Common interpretations of Buddhism go so far as to call it the root of all suffering. Could you stick anything with a greater damnation? The reasoning, a gross over-simplification of a rich and nuanced philosophy, goes as follows: Either we desire something(s) that we don't get, or we do get what we desire but find it unsatisfying. In both cases, our minds are turbulent, grasping, disappointed, unsatiated. We suffer.

Buddhists aren't alone in taking a dim view of desire. Desire, and we for engaging in it, are condemned by many other religious, philosophical, and social frameworks; the moral spectrum sharing this attitude is wide, ranging from right-wing Christians who insist on renunciation of desires, with overtones of guilt and shame adding weight to their injunctions, to, on the other end, progressives in the voluntary simplicity movement who urge us to live with less for reasons of environmental and personal health. They enjoin us to view desires as unnecessary and a societal evil, to avoid shopping, purchasing, and generally increasing the number of our possessions, to expunge greedy thoughts from our minds, to purify our lives by ridding ourselves of various material desires like a villain casting off clothing worn at the scene of a crime. Both perspectives impart a heavy moral overlay, a judgment.

What is a desire? In its simplest form, we want. Let's take Zoey as an example. She sees something, say, a piece of fish that I'm eating, tasty, redolent of salty oils and herbs. She wants it. Her desire is straightforward, visceral, and over and done with when the fish has been completely eaten, preferably some of it by her. Her desire is simple. It is finite, and it can be quelled.

When the kids are at their dad's house for the weekend, I like to spread out a placemat on our living room carpet, set the "table" for myself in this sea of low beize pile, maybe bring a candle down from table to floor to illuminate my space, sometimes even pour a glass of wine. On my scale of luxuries, the full picture feels like a radical statement of self-indulgence. I sit cross-legged, contentedly casual, and unhurried. At these times, I make a conscious practice of appreciation, which is much easier in this calm low space, by myself, than up at the table in the company of adolescents.

Zoey, a well-disciplined companion, watches patiently but intently from a short distance, secure in the knowledge that her turn will come. Her job at mealtimes is to perform the "pre-wash cycle," that is, a thorough licking of my plate after I finish eating and before I put it into the dishwasher.

While she waits her turn, her whole being, her perked up ears, focused eyes, nose twitching every so minutely, muscles tensed, fixate on my dwindling piece of salmon. She embodies desire.

Usually Zoey doesn't get table scraps, beyond the odd piece of fish skin, grains of brown rice, or cheese stuck to the plate which she manages to scrape off using a combination of teeth and determination. She knows she won't ever eat my dinner. This, however, doesn't stop her from wanting it, time and again. When food is in front of her, so close but out of reach, she is full of expectation; she sees the opportunity, experiences the desire, in its fullest.

Does Zoey *suffer* from this desire? Not a bit. She wants something, she gets (usually this means, consumes) it in whatever portion, and then the experience is over.

What, then, is so problematic for humans about desire?

Tazetta, an elementary school classmate of Sam's, once offered me a newfound insight. She had been on a trip to Florida with her divorced dad over spring break, and had just returned with a cool new toy, the latest in yo-yo technology. Yo-yos, that year, were a raging fad. Her younger sister had been at our house, on a play date with Carolyn, and now Tazetta and her dad had arrived for pick-up. While the dad retrieved his younger daughter, Tazetta proudly showed me her new acquisition, demonstrating how she could make it sleep at the bottom of a throw, or bounce twice before climbing back up its string. Her pride was nearly tangible. Then, out of the blue, she confided a recent epiphany: "The problem with getting something that you really want is that you only really want it for a little while, and then you just want something else." Bingo. An eight-year old had solved the mystery of desire, the basic force which, in itself and for the response it elicits in us, drives so much of our civilization – religion, psychology, morality, politics, and, of course, marketing.

For, unlike dogs, we humans don't let our desires play themselves out and then extinguish themselves, like a candle flame once the wick has vanished into air and ash. Supposing I hold a burger in front of Zoey. She desires it, thoroughly and urgently. Her whole body quivers with the wanting. She can barely hold still, in the "sit" pose I have commanded. I give her the burger, the object of desire. In seconds flat, she has ingested it, probably with minimal activity on the part of her teeth; Zoey has made a science of efficiency, as applied to eating. In her effort to speed up her intake, she foregoes the time-consuming and largely unnecessary step of chewing. Having polished off the burger, she looks at me as if to say, "That's gone. Is there more?" No, I show her my empty hands. She takes in this information quickly, and with that realization, it's over. Her desire is quenched, and she's ready to move on – to a walk, a nap, a chew toy, whatever appealing opportunity next presents itself. End of story.

Our human downfall comes in our tendency to *think* about our desires rather than to just have them, act on them, and release them. The story does not begin with a possibility and does not end with its fruition. We think about what we want in advance, obsessively or passingly, and sometimes for a very long time. At some point, emotion joins in the turmoil, first animating us with anticipation and a zing of excitement, vision, hope, but quickly morphing into wanting, dissatisfaction, impatience, neediness. We crave.

Consider the humble, but universally loved, chocolate chip cookie. A dog would smell a batch of freshly baked cookies, scout out the source and see them cooling on wire racks on the counter, stand on her hind paws with front paws at the counter's edge, and if lucky enough to be able to reach them, ravenously gulp them down. With gusto. Desire, vigorously alive and well, is now satisfied. By contrast, we too might approach the situation with a mix of contentment and excitement. After all, they smell so good… We take one cookie, expecting to enjoy it; but no sooner is cookie in hand than we worry about whether or not we should have indulged; we wind up eating it in thirds, conflicted; we leave the kitchen with a sneaking sense of micro-failure, but return, drawn to the site of the original crime, nagged by the call of the next cookie; wavering on the edge of indecision, we sweep up a few crumbs from the counter, break a tiny piece from a third cookie (a misshapen one, we rationalize), or lick the batter from the edge of the mixing bowl, surreptitiously. Batter, of course, doesn't count; no matter how much we eat, we justify, it is not a cookie. Once we have navigated an intense debate (Woman vs. Cookie), we immerse ourselves in guilt and remorse, making resolutions and planning in anticipation how we will handle such challenges in the future. Ingeniously, we create an entire drama out of what, for a dog, constitutes a one-minute affair. But it is the dog whose pleasure is pure.

Often it is the attachment to our desire, rather than the desire itself, that causes us to suffer. The nature of that guise of suffering, the suffering of attachment, is mental turbulence in its myriad forms. Wanting, planning, wishing, needing, comparing, feeling worthy or unworthy, over-attaching and feeling addicted; these all divert us from the simple process of desiring, enjoying the desired thing while we have it, and moving onward after the enjoyment.

This logic – letting go of attachment, and thereby enjoying more, struggling less – it turns out, is far easier to apply to a chocolate chip cookie than to a life. Zoey's life, for one. I have an intense desire, which is for her continued physical presence, her adorable body, her quizzical face, her wiggles and wriggles on her back, her wild dashes about the house, her companionship. There are corollary desires: I want her not to endure pain, and not to lose function. I fast forward in my mind to her loss, and because I do so, undeniably, in full heartbreak, I suffer. If I could release this desire, would I? Honestly, no. This pain, though rooted in attachment and not yet necessary, in a strange and paradoxical way confirms my love. I wouldn't have it otherwise.

One of my favorite spiritual teachers (Deepak Chopra)[1] says, a radical departure on the face of it, that there's nothing *wrong* with desire, in fact, it's the most natural of human emotions. In his view, our birthright is not to fight desire, but to have our desires spontaneously fulfilled. "Spontaneous," here, is the operative word. A desire – be it a thing, person, event, experience – arises, we meet it, and we are fulfilled. In this natural process, we feel happiness. This teacher assures us that it is fine, and not a marker of our moral inferiority, to experience a continual stream of desires, and that it is perfectly alright to enjoy the succession of their fulfillments. Our role is to let go and "let the universe take care of the details," and as long as we are happy in this process, abundance flows and all is well. What does it mean to be happy through the iterative process of desire and fulfillment? We must detach from the outcome, relinquish the effort to make things happen, allow the present just to be, and let the Universe work its magic. In this way, things continuously come to us, all intended for our enjoyment.

Another very popular spiritual teacher (Eckhard Tolle)[2] agrees that simply to be, to be in a state of peace with whatever exists right now, is the key to happiness. He

---

[1] I acknowledge that this is a gross over-simplification of Chopra's ideas, and does not sufficiently represent his brilliance and insight.

[2] I acknowledge that this is a gross over-simplification of Tolle's ideas, and does not sufficiently represent his wisdom.

appears around the world at retreats, conferences, book signings with, in his own words, "nothing to say." He makes a single point, for which seekers are willing to travel far and wide, to collectively spend millions of dollars on books and audio-recordings. The message they quest to hear couldn't be more basic: There is nothing but Now. Not only does our tendency to continually review the past or to worry about the future cause us to suffer, it also focuses us on a complete fiction. In dwelling on something other than the present, we are focusing on something that does not now, never has, and never will exist. Only the Now exists. Quite fortunately, being rooted in the present moment, freeing our minds from all other imagined or recollected times, allows the mind to tranquilly rest. I recently checked the latest of Tolle's workshops, captured on CD, out of the Chapel Hill Public Library; it contains many expanses of silence, likely to illustrate his point.

Many people like to train their dogs through obedience classes or other formalized programs, as if acculturating their pets to life in human society, simultaneously positioning themselves as responsible dog owners. Obedience, in dogs, has undeniable advantages. I once took on the job of dog-sitting for my boss, welcoming her two large dogs into my home for the two-week duration of her vacation. Both of these dogs were, at that time, hugely oversized puppies weighing upwards of sixty pounds.

My boss, a self-professed "alpha dog" herself, has a long history of big dogs; of necessity, she knows how to establish excellent canine control. These two pups, however, were new to her family. The younger, Archie, had only recently transitioned from the shelter to their home. Tall and lanky, he still wore a spiked choke collar, resembling either an instrument of torture or a punk rocker's concept of accessorizing, to make him more manageable on a leash. Valentine, the older though still adolescent, towered a couple inches above Archie, exuberant in her greetings and wild in her tussles with Archie. The two of them dashed around the house and yard, almost visibly shrinking the size of our indoor and outdoor spaces by their ability to cover ground in the blink of an eye.

At 5:00 a.m. on the first morning of their stay, I donned my running shoes, ready to exercise these friendly, playful, and giant guests. Zoey slumbered peacefully under Carolyn's covers. Leashes and collars in hand, I opened the door to Archie's crate while Valentine, a large blondish lab mix with undeniable Greyhound influence, pranced expectantly, bubbling with energy and eager to run. Together, now collared and leashed, the twosome dragged me downstairs, my legs barely keeping up with the pull on my upper body and my bleary mind alarmed at the demand, exceeding what I could ordinarily manage at that hour. Their sense of direction was immediate: to the back door, the closest exit! I looped the leashes around my wrist to make sure I could keep my grasp, and pushed the button to raise the automatic garage door, that barrier between inside and freedom. Little did I know that the neighbors' cat, Sparky, sat in our driveway just a few feet away, on the other side of the garage door. This fact had not eluded the dogs, not for even a split second.

Archie moved first, taking off at full speed after Sparky; Sparky dashed across the street, disappearing behind the neighbor's house. Thrilled for a chase, driven by pure impulse, Archie charged full-speed ahead, with me helplessly in tow, an afterthought, attached to his forward motion by the tenuous connection of a leash. My legs scrambled to keep up once again as my body catapulted forward; a massive surge of adrenalin flooded my system like electricity. A yell escaped me, a reaction of panic and utter out-of-control-ness. This caught Archie's attention, causing him to pull up short and allowing me to regain control. I reined him in, and re-gathered Valentine's leash as well. Yes, behavior training has huge advantages for a dog's human companions.

As a puppy, we taught Zoey to "come," along with commands for sit, paw, lie down, and roll over. Zoey, a clever pup, maintained an attitude of choice, of selectivity, about these behaviors. In any given instance, when asked to execute one of her "tricks," she performed a quick cost/benefit analysis. The result determined whether or not she would obey. A common scenario begins with the simple command. She might, for example, have slipped through the back door and be standing in the driveway. One of us calls to her, "Zoey, come!" in hopes of averting a lengthy disappearance (to her, an adventure), which might postpone our trip to the pool. Zoey considers, "Would I rather earn a treat by coming to this call, or enjoy a free run outside, and a little time to explore?" Our odds are, at best, fifty-fifty.

Mealtimes, with the immediate promise of reward, of desire and fulfillment, presented a convenient time for practicing Zoey's commands. "Sit... lie down... roll over." We made, and continue to uphold, an agreement: If she complies, we deliver her food bowl, complete with a scoop of kibbles. Always eager to get right on with the business of eating, Zoey honed her speed of execution, to the point that sitliedownrollover became one seamless movement. She could glide from standing through sitting to a semi-prone position, a molten blur, then quickly wriggle around and stand up again, in a split second. A good deal of form was compromised for the sake of velocity, in her effort to get to the real interest at hand, food. Unwittingly, we had trained her to anticipate, to rush through the present moment, to focus on the future, in short, to desire – in our human, goal-driven way, with outcome and pay-off eclipsing process and present.

Infuriating as it is, I have to honor Zoey's choice to enjoy running freely, joyfully, even defiantly, across our yard and through the neighborhood rather than to obey our firm, insistent, "come." She's living completely in her present moment, relishing it to the fullest, wanting nothing other than what she is experiencing. She has met her desire head-on, and milked it for its true and fitting reward – happiness. She has even weighed it against a competing desire, a doggie cookie, made her choice and completely immersed herself in it without any second thoughts. Without retrospective regret, she even seems to enjoy her own defiance.

Invariably, Zoey tires herself out from exuberant exertion, and a half hour later, we'll hear a scratch at the front door. Her desire for outdoor freedom has burnt itself out, cleanly, leaving no ash. Innocently her eyes beseech us, Can I still have my treat?

I also have a cat. This, I admit to as a Dog Person, though Yammy actually preceded Zoey by about a year. The cat was the pilot pet, testing the waters to determine whether my three- and six-year-old children were "pet ready." The answer, in a word, was "no."

Yammy arrived out of urgency; we responded to a call for rescue. Having learned that this gregarious kitty would be euthanized in one more day if no one claimed him, a family in Carolyn's Montessori preschool had temporarily adopted him from the animal shelter, providing a safe way station. While they couldn't take on a pet themselves – they were in the process of moving out of state – they also couldn't bear to see such a friendly animal put to death. The presence of a preschooler no doubt helped the cause, though I have to wonder why they were window-shopping at the animal shelter so close to their own relocation. Anyway, they sent an emergency plea out to the class parents and I, an animal lover, soft-hearted, and generally eager to help, responded.

On first sight, Yammy was a veritable mess. Fur matted, scrawny, filthy, he wasn't going anywhere on visual appeal. He held a trump card though, in his personality. One of those naturally extroverted, amiable, long-furred, floppy, orange cats, he is a walking stereotype – the quintessential gregarious tomcat. He makes friends easily and "plays well with others," at least human others. With fellow felines, he's a holy terror.

As an adolescent and an animal in new surroundings, Yammy needed attention. Substantial attention. At this point in my life, the many guises of "attending to" seemed to be my entire raison d'etre. I attended to all day long, whether to the kids and their needs, to my husband and his, or to the house and yard, and theirs. Yammy's arrival added one more entity with needs, and I did my best to juggle his attention with reading children's books, piecing together squishy puzzles, coloring, cutting toasted bagels into bit-sized pieces for snack. It was a tough mix which I managed with some difficulty; the younger of my two children made no secret of her jealousy. If Yammy wanted to play kitty fishing, me casting the line with a catnip-stuffed fish, him chasing and pouncing and rolling over and over with his catch, Carolyn would pull the fishing rod right out of my hand, her point being, my attention belonged to *her*, on her book or puzzle or game. In this experience with cat/family integration, the message was clear – we purely and simply were not puppy-ready.

By the next summer, Yammy had settled in and the kids had added another couple inches each, presumably maturing another year along with their increases in height and shoe size. We were approaching a pivotal point, the time for bringing home a puppy. On summer vacation with my family in Maine, while tending to children on the beach, I read puppy training books with the same excited anticipation as a would-be traveler devouring color, glossy, travel brochures and guidebooks. I planned and prepared, considered the advantages of crates, studied house training methods, wondered whether I could manage the rigors of teaching obedience. And then, with school back in session and the endless "vacation" mercifully over, I mentioned our plan to adopt a puppy to a workman; we had covered just about every topic by this point, given the quantity of measuring and sawing and hammering involved in replacing rotted trim around all of our windows with fresh wood. As luck would have it, a neighbor of his was trying to "place" a whole litter of puppies, seven small pups desperately needed a good home, immediately. My heart melted into a liquidy pool of willingness. I, for one, was ready.

The night before we planned to pick up our new baby dog, Hurricane Fran struck Chapel Hill. We had seen nothing of our newest family member, not even a photo. These days, every animal available for adoption at the shelters has a picture and a personality profile posted on the web (much like internet dating, actually); back then, we had only a verbal description, provided over the phone by a mom, much like me I imagine, all too ready to whittle back her responsibilities. And we had a street address, and a date and time arranged for meeting the puppy and, if all went well, taking her home with us.

That night, wildly destructive winds tore through Chapel Hill, and rain pelted down like a cascade of bullets, shot at an angle, sometimes nearly sideways, pelting the side of the house. Dawn brought with it a morning-after hush, no one outdoors, damages not yet assessed, power off, the town quiet as if stunned. Although the storm had wreaked havoc in our neighborhood, devastating the trees and power lines, we had little idea of the extent of its destruction. We climbed into our green Honda and headed out as planned, abuzz with anticipation. We made it out of our neighborhood, veering around branches and power lines draped loosely across the concrete sidewalks and pavement. Downed trees and power lines blocked numerous routes, impeding progress through physical obstruction and implicit harm, respectively. Portions of the region lost electricity for weeks; our neighborhood struggled along without air conditioning, light, or refrigeration for nine sweltering September days.

The puppy mission called, notwithstanding. Wending our way across town, inching along at well below even the most conservative in-town speed limit, we managed to find the house. Since our phone had gone dead, the line severed somewhere and probably in multiple places, we hadn't been able to call. (This was before the advent of cell phones.) The family met use with surprise at the door. Come in! (Subtext, are you crazy?!)

Zoey's mother had been properly named, we were assured. I imagine she had started life with a name like Camille, for a Southern lady, or perhaps Dixie; she had been acculturated in a modest southern home, was surely accustomed to the local accent, having grown up in the rural outskirts of this North Carolina county. She had probably chewed her share of greasy small bones, the remnants of fried chicken. By this point, however, whatever semblance of a respectable dog name she had once borne had been jettisoned in favor of "Sweet Thing," employed by her owners to better reflect her character. I took this as an excellent sign; I'd read that, in choosing a puppy, one should pay special attention to the maternal character. Like mother, like pup.

Sweet Thing was smaller than I expected, and skinny, her ribs covered by the merest film of skin, only her thin fur preventing transparency, her haunches gaunt. She was lying on a dirty towel spread out over a concrete floor, in the corner of a simple tin-roofed carport, where she sheltered several tiny baby dogs – seven living beings, together a theme and variation in black and white fluff. Their rounded, fragile, fuzzy presence seemed incongruous with their setting, against the stark backdrop, a hard gray surface. One pup caught my eye, the last remaining daughter, I was told. She was tiny, making her coat – a baby cow suit that could serve her well for puppy Halloween – all the more cute, and a tad ridiculous. On the ride home, the four of us (two parents, two kids fighting over rights to hold the pup) had a lively discussion about names. With a white stripe between the two black halves of her face, she nearly escaped being called Oreo. Referencing J.D. Salinger's *Franny and Zoey*, an obscure nod to the natural disaster that marked her arrival in our family, I prevailed over the kids' suggestion. Zoey, she became.

Dogs and cats make entirely different claims on their humans. Yammy, as an adult, seeks us out on his schedule. We cater to him, letting him in and out at his whim, feeding him when he asks, patting him when he chooses to nuzzle or nestle. He gratifies us with his affection, but he, the cat, holds the reins. It is we who come to him, at his behest.

Zoey, by contrast, approaches us on our terms. We decide when she will walk, eat, be patted. She is happy with this arrangement, agreeing to our plans without complaint as if there were no other. She is an unabashed people-pleaser, happy when we are happy, consoling when we are sad, affectionate when we wish to be so with her. In short, she erects no barriers to the free flow of love.

One would think that, since we all want love, giving and receiving it would come rather naturally, like breathing. Love, like oxygen, can be taken for granted, but unlike the air we breathe, love makes its presence known; it stays in our awareness, and often with a sense of not-enough-ness. We want more. With oxygen, we arrive at an easy point where we feel satiated and have enough; with love, though, we assume that more is better. You might suspect that people would overdo it, trying to increase the flow of love rather than impede it. I find it's actually quite the reverse – all too often, we have trouble giving and receiving love, we block its flow instead of welcoming it, and we suffer as a result.

My daughter, Carolyn, is a girl with a sense of fun, a brilliant mind, musical talent, natural athletic ability, and confidence in her abilities. She has many friends, and to her credit they display a wide range of characteristics (including intelligence) and maturity levels. Today, she is what I would consider "easy," making few demands, seeming happy and well-adjusted, doing well in everything. But as an infant, she challenged me – specifically, my inner mom, the nurturer. I wanted to hold her close; she pushed me away. While other mothers had little girls who would cuddle and hug, my beloved daughter insisted on standing apart. She had no interest in participating in a sweet, lovey-dovey, baby girl/mom rapport. I suffered pangs of disappointment. She wriggled at best, and often bristled, when hugged, refused to humor me with "I wuv you." Ironically, though, when others tried to get close to her – to ask a question or deliver a kiss – it was me to whom she fled for safe haven.

By nature, from the day she was born, Carolyn avoided sentimentality in all its guises. Where does this tendency come from, in such a small child? Are we brainwashed in thinking that all children want to love and be loved? What makes one child soften in your arms, like warm putty conforming to your body, but another stiffen and squirm away? This remains a mystery, one of those things that it's best to accept as is, without excuse, explanation, or comparison. But I understand the impulse to shrink back, to *not* connect. I, too, over the course of my childhood had constructed walls of self-judgment and protection around me. It took me the better part of three decades to get to the point where I could gradually dismantle them, a deconstruction which required great effort and courage.

My son, as an infant, toddler, and little boy, began life with quite the reverse attitude about loving. This was a saving grace, as it allowed me to believe that I was not responsible for Carolyn's sometimes embarrassing responses. A mother's dream, little Sam had thrived on closeness, and specifically, the intimacy of his relationship with his mom. From an early age, he articulated his feelings, doling out a natural sweetness and love that I found, daily, amazing. Unlike his sister, he began in the flow, giving and receiving love with simple joy.

And then, adolescence hit, full force. Depression had been gradually building within him over several years; I regret that I didn't realize the storms brewing inside him until they approached gale, and intermittently hurricane, force. I had thought, wishfully, that the havoc wreaked by his troubled relationship with his father would diminish over time, like the gradual calming of a churned up ocean, but I underestimated the wreckage that had already taken place, and the aftermath. Descending into a morass of fourteen-year-old self-loathing, he actively shut me out of his inner world. The flow ceased.

I understand my son's walls too. I began my first career in Self-Hatred early in childhood; I remember a plaguing sense of unlovability as far back as kindergarten. By elementary school, I harbored horrible secrets about myself which I nearly, but never quite, told my closest friends. I carefully scripted confessions, practiced in my mind describing this most intimate reality and the over-riding force in my life, though I never did summon the courage to deliver my practiced speeches. As an adolescent, I became remote, reclusive, and haggard. I imagine that I was not the most pleasant being to live with, after all, it was hard enough for me to get along with my self – how could I expect others to appreciate me, to react positively or even gravitate toward me? (I imagine my son won't remember himself as a frighteningly belligerent, either.)

As a teenager, with no one to remind – or at this point, convince – me of my own worth, I strove to obliterate my loathsome self. As a college freshman, I was drawn to Buddhism for its portrayal of the self as illusion; I warped it, however, to suit my own purposes, focusing on the experience of no-self and forgetting the anchor of happiness and compassion at its core. In those days, I probably couldn't have received love even if someone offered it up to me on a silver platter, for there was nothing inside me to recognize love, to resonate with it. To accept love, of course, you must first be able to see it before you, and trust that the offer is genuine. I lacked this capacity.

How do you teach another person, young or old or anywhere in between, to allow love in? There is a prerequisite, an intermediate step without which love cannot be received, and which is arguably our hardest task in this lifetime. It is to fall in love with ourselves, without shame or guilt, without pride or arrogance, but with a deep compassion for who we have been and a deep appreciation for who we are becoming. For we must allow love *within* ourselves before we are able to permit love from the outside to come in, before we can receive and accept the love offered by others. When we have learned the art of self-love, we are grounded in the confidence that we have all the love we need, within ourselves, a wellspring. Only then can we receive from others the love that will replenish us, so that we can truly, without strings or conditions, give it back.

Dogs know this. They accept love and return it, or conversely, they give it and then receive in return. It is an easy, effortless exchange, like breathing in and out, out and in. Humans have to learn this. We harbor from the outset, or we develop, a fear of judgment, or non-reciprocation, or neediness, or vulnerability, and these stand in the way of our receiving and giving love. Though they may not seem so on the surface, they are all variations of pride, and they hold us back, impeding our freedom and our happiness.

Dogs, never immersed in an individualized sense of self and thus devoid of pride, occupy a loving world. Their minds don't dwell on, well, on their minds, with its separate troubles, wishes, anxieties. Hence, for the dog, the myriad issues that stand between us and love never arise. We would do well to take note. How do we become more capable of love, more able to give and receive it? First by examining our foibles, those individualized barriers to love – who we think we are, how we believe others see us, how we feel about ourselves, and the repercussions of these beliefs. Then, by recognizing these facets of our personality, these descriptions of our unique reality, as masks for pride – the absorption in self, whether through positive or negative lenses. Once exposed, we can make a daring choice – we can drop these masks. Though this decision may seem like a form of self-negation, in fact it is quite the opposite. It is our recognition of a greater Self, which is also us, but which lies beyond the ways and wiles of the personality. Aligning with this unencumbered being-ness, we can allow ourselves the simple pleasure of living in a loving world.

What if dogs labeled each other? Humans do, after all, and constantly. We no sooner meet someone than a host of descriptors ricochet through our minds: gender, size, shape, race, for starters. We progress to subtler levels fairly quickly: intelligence, education level, socio-economic background, details of appearance. Peeling back further, we differentiate: fit or out-of-shape, quick-witted or average, good-natured or arrogant, awkward or poised, confident or timid, mensch or egotist. In a matter of seconds, we sum up total strangers in a multidimensional matrix of measures. Usually, this process is automatic, often unconscious.

Zoey, by contrast, does none of this categorizing. This is not for lack of indexes; with hundreds of breeds, a huge variety of canine phenotypes, and as broad a spectrum of individual backgrounds as humans have, dogs could easily classify one another. *If* they were so inclined. (We'll leave capability out of the picture for the moment.)

Our classifications of people serve several purposes, not the least of which is to define our place in the world. Dividing individuals into groups enables us to identify which group we belong to, a process which can support belonging and connection; its dark side is exclusion and bigotry. Ranking within our categories allows us to know where we stand, another dubious form of security with a dark side in superiority. For example, a primary axis of classification is physical appearance – which in humans encompasses everything from shape to size to physical features to color of hair and skin. We can place ourselves within a category, females in their forties, for example, and then size ourselves up against others in the same class.

Dogs are at a distinct disadvantage here, for it is much harder for them to compare themselves to others based on physical appearance. The sheer number of dog breeds, and the huge variety among breeds, not to mention the scattershot diversity of mutts, would make it nearly impossible for any dog to make appearance-based judgments. And if the occasional canine did try to categorize his or her peers, and to judge them as superior or inferior based on this measure, well, that snobbery could only cause suffering. There simply isn't enough homogeneity to support it. Consider the lone representative of, say, the Outer Hebrides Terrier breed living in Chapel Hill, NC. He'd find himself isolated and unsupported if he chose to engage in canine racism, associating with and thinking highly of only his own breed.

When Zoey was three years old and my kids had both started elementary school, I began working part-time for a faculty member in Maternal and Child Health at the local university. Though I had been out of the workforce for almost a decade, the connection was clinched by the fact that Dot – a well-funded, doctorally trained, successful academic, incidentally Black – and I had gone to the same graduate program in public health. My role was to manage Dot's small non-profit, a spin-off which she created in order to design and evaluate programs for at-risk adolescents. Drugs, pregnancy, and communicable diseases were the big three issues, each fueled by drop-out and poverty and largely impacting minorities.

In an ironic twist of fate, the renovated tobacco warehouses in downtown Durham provided space for our office as well as for TROSA (Transitional Rehabilitation of Substance Abusers), a community fixture and admirable organization. Founded by a recovered addict dedicated to giving back to others with similar struggles, TROSA takes in some of our community's most desperate men and, through an intensive and demanding two-year program, returns them to their own lives, with a new outlook, vision, skills, and capacity to function. Many of the program's participants do make this transition, and excellently.

TROSA participants staffed Building #7, in which I worked for my first two years back in the workforce. They served as front desk attendants, security personnel, and maintenance and janitorial staff. Labels, reflecting various stances, would have been easy to come by for this group of individuals: addict (pseudo-clinical, blaming), derelict (superior, shaming), pitiful/poor (empathic, elitist), welfare case (classist, pseudo-liberal), down-and-out (dismissive). The overwhelming majority of program participants, 100% as I remember things, were Black.

The friendliness and professionalism of the TROSA men, however, could have eroded these sorts of judgment in even an unabashed racist. These guys made coffee, opened doors, greeted, assisted, walked the hallways, changed light bulbs, monitored the parking lot – with dedication and decided pleasantness. They were on their way up. Never mind that it was a boulder-strewn path, with hairpin bends, ups and downs, and many false summits.

Most days, I enjoyed a work break every now and then, when one or another would drop by my office, really more of a cubicle, for a talk. The stories I heard, the personal histories of these exemplary individuals, would have sounded the death knell for any listener's lingering racist sentiments. Their starkness leaves no room for cognitive dissonance; at times, it is simply not possible to simultaneously understand the backdrop to a life, and condemn the individual for subsequent errors of judgment or behavior.

I remember Jimmy's story as the most heart-wrenching. I had known Jimmy for about six months before he told me anything about his background. Until that point, he had steered conversations away from anything related to his family or personal life, and had divulged next to nothing about his past. I deferred to his choice, not pressing the issue in favor of allowing him to connect with others (especially a white woman, working a white-collar job) within his comfort zone. Little did I know…

One day, after a pause in our friendly daily banter about this and that, Jimmy quietly announced that he was ready to tell me his story. Only me. He was clear about this privacy, explicit that he was about to divulge stuff that he did not, emphatically did not, want just anybody to know. I accepted his trust as an honor.

Jimmy came from one of those large southern families which spread, like a web of belonging and identity, across North Carolina. Some have grown to gerimander adjacent states, often Virginia or Georgia. The bonds between family members remained tight, despite enlarging geographic distances. To keep up with one another, Jimmy's entire extended family came together every June in a three- or four-day family reunion, a rejoining around babies and children, shared histories, updates of circumstances and activities, new spouses, new jobs. They pitched in on a giant barbecue, which in the South means something very specific: pulled pork, ribs, corn, butter beans, cole slaw, potato salad, banana pudding (yes, the sort made with slices of banana, bright yellow instant pudding, and vanilla wafers, topped with whipped "cream" most likely squirted from a can). The color green is blatantly absent at a Southern barbecue, as are the hot dogs and hamburgers which a Northerner like me associates with a "cook-out." Principal activities are visiting and, the feature, "setting" (translation: sitting). A couple hundred of Jimmy's family members gathered each summer; usually, those who traveled to the event squeezed onto couches, slept on floors in sleeping bags, or lived out of rented campers.

One summer, Jimmy and his cousins who lived nearby decided that they'd do up the next year's reunion in style. On inspiration, they pooled their money and bought a foreclosure, an entire small motel that had gone bankrupt. For months, they cleaned, painted, and repaired the vacant, somewhat dilapidated, building, preparing it to house two hundred close and distant family members – all in one place, instead of dispersed across numerous homes and stuffed into cramped quarters. Spirits were soaring. This would be the best reunion ever! The building inspector came; all was acceptable except, he cautioned, don't overtax the electrical system.

Family members arrived and were delighted with the upgraded accommodations; the reunion planners were proud; suitcases were carried up stairs and rooms were claimed; all was unfolding beautifully. Although they lived locally, Jimmy moved his family, his wife and four children, into motel rooms to be close to the others. It was, after all, a big party, a Reunion. He spent the afternoon welcoming the newly arrived and lugging baggage out of car trunks, up stairs, into proudly presented rooms.

As evening approached, the temperature began to drop. Sometimes, in the South, we have uncharacteristically chilly nights at the very beginning of summer; the air has not yet thickened to its densely humid July and August state, and its comparative dryness allows for a large temperature gradient as day dissolves into night. Envisioning relatives shivering in their rooms, the event organizers, Jimmy among them, warned everyone not to plug in anything electrical, especially not space heaters, which some had packed into their trunks alongside extra coolers, folding lawn chairs, baseball bats and footballs.

It was nearly nine o'clock when darkness fell. Jimmy headed out to pick up a bite to eat, and to give himself a break from the afternoon's exertions. Maybe he hung out with some friends, maybe he went to a bar for a cold beer. Anyway, a couple hours passed and, late at night, he drove back to the motel. Even before the building came into view, sirens pierced his consciousness, then glaring lights shattered the dark. As he neared the scene, a horrifying realization dawned up him, that the sounds, the thickening smoke, the flashing lights were coming from their renovated motel. In the heightened, surreal, state of mind one has when living a nightmare, he arrived at the scene as rescue workers removed bodies from the building and covered with them sheets, body after body. He counted ten before losing track. In all, forty-two family members died in that fire, including Jimmy's wife and children.

Stunned, Jimmy got back in his car. What else was there to do? He drove and drove and drove. Who knows where? Not Jimmy. In a state of utter shock, one which words could never capture, beside which our most horrible imaginings turn pale, he just kept going. He might have been driving for days, he told me. From there, the picture gets fuzzy. For the ten-odd years between his escape from the inferno and his retelling of this story to me, he numbed himself with drugs, day and night. This part is easy to understand. What is amazing and less fathomable is not that he succumbed to drugs, but that he somehow found the strength and the desire to pull himself out of a total and complete morass, a black hole of the soul.

Could anyone, after hearing this story, continue to label Jimmy? An addict, subsisting on drugs, for a major portion of his life? An idiot, for not confiscating the space heaters as his family arrived? Weakling, for allowing himself to relinquish all self-control to drugs? Coward, for fleeing the scene? When levied in light of his story, these judgments become absurd, untenable. Compassion shows them up for what they are – petty, shallow, and ignorant.

All of the TROSA men have a history. Though not all of their stories are as horrific as Jimmy's, they are all compelling, and they all deserve a surge of compassion.

If we are honest, each one of us will admit that we are, in some degree, guilty of labeling. It is instantaneous, often unwitting, reflexive; akin to what Malcolm Gladwell termed "thin slicing," it is simply one of the ways in which our brains process new stimuli. When this information is a new person in front of us, our snap judgments depart from the benign, they become potentially damaging. But our minds, too, have the capacity for reflection and course correction; we can review our initial labeling and – if unjust or unkind, or even just unnecessary, adding unproductive negativity to the world – we can over-ride it. We need to back up, to weld together those thin slices into a thick slab better approximating an actual living being, a person with a deep history. If we could just hear, sometimes only possible through inference and understanding, the stories of the people whom we label, I do believe we would witness an end to prejudice of all sorts.

During that same time period, while I was working in Building #7 of downtown Durham's former tobacco warehouses, our little non-profit (and more specifically, I) weathered an unpleasant incident. Errors were made in the organization's book-keeping. Someone, we never knew who, accused Gertie, a spry, quick-tongued, Black woman who worked for the organization in various administrative capacities. Gertie, whom I knew only passingly, suspected me of implicating her; in confidence, she advised the organization's director and my boss, Dot, that "maybe it was a racist thing." (As a goy, I had learned from my Jewish ex-mother-in-law that the axe of labeling cuts both ways.) Dot, not one to mince words, gave Gertie an instant and indignant upbraiding. "Jane hasn't got a racist bone in her body!" Also one for full transparency, she reported this scene to me, case closed. I still consider this one of the greatest compliments I've ever received.

Though bruised and disappointed at being called a racist, I couldn't be angry with Gertie. She, too, had a story. One year ago, at age 58 and as a single working woman, she had adopted a crack baby, one not even related to her. In the months that I knew her, she was juggling work, child care, church, and the numerous medical requirements of an infant addict, with a matter-of-fact sense of determination and purpose. Impressive, and beyond label.

As people, the culture that they create, and the society that houses them change, and as we become more sophisticated and fine-tuned in our assessments, labels evolve. I now work with a woman who makes liberal use of the term "Big Dog Person," and prides herself in being one. She describes others, with overt undertones of camaraderie, as Big Dog People, including them in this implicitly-bonded, arguably self-congratulatory, club. I'm not sure what the attributes are that differentiate these sorts of people from the rest of us humble small- and mid-sized dog persons, or non-dog-owners for that matter, but it's clear that they're all positive. I find myself, the owner of a merely 25-pound dog, on the outside.

What is the purpose of this, or any, label? To be sure, it evokes feelings of inclusion, of bonds based on shared attributes or values or background. As if enveloped in old and comfortable clothing, we recognize the warmth and security conveyed by a sense of belonging. But at what cost? Labels that bind and include have an alter-ego, expressions of a shadow side – they are easily morphed into distinctions that stigmatize and exclude. Individuals experience these by-products, sometimes inadvertent, sometimes consciously promoted, in emotionally painful ways. On a societal scale, groups of people experience them as tribalism and bigotry.

One little known fact, hidden deep in the basement of my past, is that, as a young girl, I was a Horse Lover. I use the word "fact" as a tepid understatement, for while other girls are drawn to horses, obsess about them, fill their lives with all things horse-related, I was head over heels in love. I remember one night when my parents had invited my father's tennis coach, Arnie, over for dinner. The subject of horses came up in conversation, who knows how, and I most likely let out some sort of heartstring-pulling whimper, a plaintive pining. "Does Jane like horses?" Arnie asked, innocently, making an effort to include a six-year-old in the conversation. "Is the sky blue? Is the grass green? *Does Jane like horses??*" my father responded. Apparently I had gotten my message across.

For kids, summer in New England, and possibly in other parts of the country, means camp. Our family with four kids couldn't afford sleep-away camps (or so we believed), but day camp, generally selected by my mother, was a simple fact of life. It typically involved swimming lessons, a prospect which sent terror as a shiver through my entire being; I was, shall we say, a fearful child and swimming lessons ranked high among the objects of fear. Fortunately, other activities which came easily for me – archery, for instance, which involved no competition and no teamwork, with its potential for ostracism – made day camp a mixed bag. However, it was not a choice, but just what we did, as much a part of summer as popsicles or weeding the garden.

And then, on the Christmas of my twelfth year, I got an unusual present – an IOU card promising two weeks of horse-back riding camp, a day camp still, but entirely focused on horses. I was ecstatic.

The summer months rolled around and with it, the start of my camp session. I borrowed the rounded, black velvet-covered, helmet, wore simple work-type boots in lieu of actual riding boots, and, instead of jodhpurs or breeches, blue jeans, long pants to avoid chafing against the smooth leather of an English saddle. Each of ten girls was assigned to a horse (Thunder was mine) for the full week, with responsibility for mucking out his or her stall, feeding, grooming with stiff brushes and curry comb, cleaning tack, exercising, riding, and cooling down after a workout in the ring. We learned to trot – sitting and posting – to canter, to jump over cavaletti and various sorts of low rails. At the end of each week, the camp staged a Horse Show, in which we displayed our riding skills and command of our horse. It was blue ribbons all around for me, both weeks, which gave a huge boost to my pride and happiness. There was also, separately for just the girls (not surprisingly, we were all girls), a closure ceremony with camper awards, one for everyone, designated by the camp's riding instructors. They turned these awards into official-looking paper certificates, cheaply calligraphic, and signed with flourish. Most lauded the camper for being "Best Sport," "Most Improved," "Best Team Spirit," "Best Sense of Humor," or some such. Mine? "Most Self-Reliant."

I was not pleased; to me, it was a covert insult, a backhanded compliment, a sting. For it meant that I was single, not one of but one apart, the implication being that I had not been embraced in the fold of horse girl society, of riding camp community. I stashed the award carefully in my camp bag, not mentioning it when I jumped out of the camp van for the last time and passed by my mother in the kitchen on the way to my bedroom. Not quite bold enough to tear the paper certificate to shreds, I hid it in the bottom of a desk drawer under a stack of miscellaneous papers, old birthday cards, school reports. At a safe time, I don't remember exactly when, I retrieved this patch of shame, crumpled it, and put it in the tall garage trash can.

Our culture boasts a long tradition of glorifying self-reliance as a core value, as American as apple pie; the tradition stretches back to the early days of New England, to the Transcendentalists whom every school child comes to know, Henry David Thoreau and Ralph Waldo Emerson. In truth, these philosophers were highly spiritual in orientation, and thus in their understanding of what it means to be self-reliant, to be self-referencing in perspective, to determine one's values and way of being by introspection, contemplation, reflection, and not by societal pressures or conformances. We, however, tend to think of self-reliance in psychological terms; someone is self-reliant if they don't need others, if they are an island, not a piece of the main.

That peculiar (a bit embarrassing) bastion of American media, the Western, takes self-reliance as a psychological trait and runs with it, at a gallop glamorizing the concept with images of pioneer, lone ranger, and cowboy, all complete unto themselves.

Is this really a good thing? Do we really *want* to not need others? My award for self-reliance, I felt, assigned me to a sidebar, placed me outside of the group, the mesh of others who supported and relied upon and enjoyed one another, who hung together, who belonged. Self-reliance, thus, looked to me not like a strength, but like a stain, a mark of difference that held me apart from others.

Is there anyone among us who, in their heart of hearts, really wants to die alone – in either the little daily ways, or the final end of life? In times that are not dire, that involve joy rather than suffering, who among us wants to *live* alone, whether alone in a sea of others, or in physical solitude? I would hazard a guess, no one.

Perhaps our task, as we become more evolved, is to build sufficient strength so that we can join and include and belong ourselves among others in the broadest sense, because of *who,* not what, we – and they – are. Or maybe even more expansively, just plain because we *are.* We don't need to rely on common descriptors for our security, nor do our bonds with others need be based on attributes of any sort, for even the positive and wholesome, like creamy raw milk, can turn sour. Ethnicity is the obvious example of a label with value, true, but all too often devolving in a way that incurs over-riding damages; religion is a close second. How many political divisions, how many wars, arise from these two methods of delineating between people, of defining "us" as opposed to "them"? Surely the positives – membership, inclusion, self-worth, and a sense of one's place in the world – can't justify the harm these labels, and the bonds they establish, incur.

I return to compassion, to the leveling power of people's stories, and to the notion, however idealistic, that we must strive to have love be our motivation, in every moment, every effort, every interaction. To the extent that we face the world with an open heart, that we enter every encounter with love, labels, with their corresponding judgments and divisions, evaporate.

*M*etaphorically, I am bracing myself for a change of season. My son leaves for college in a mere two years; my daughter, two years after that. I'm taken aback by how suddenly, after an infinity of family time, like the summer of my life, fall is drawing near and with it, the end of the parenting phase. There is a wistfulness about fall approaching, and about the end of parenting, too; it would be easy, but pointless, to lapse into anticipatory nostalgia.

I'll confess that I have already thought ahead to what it will be like, just me, without kids at the dinner table, stuffing backpacks for their school day as I get dressed for work, generating laundry at every turn, traipsing through the house after school with friends, as if on a covert mission, dutifully practicing piano and cello at the appointed times, making their endless plans for things big and small, unprioritized.

My visions of the post-parenting phase have always included Zoey. Zoey would wait for me while I'm at work, and greet me when I came home to a childless house. We would become very close, like an elderly couple, relying on each other exclusively, in those future days. We'd spend together, just her and me, the endless stretch of days marching on into the distance, like dominoes lined up indefinitely, waiting to fall in succession. Until, when college vacations rolled around, she'd be overjoyed to welcome two much-matured and nearly independent kids back to their home. And I would take up residency once again in the kitchen.

Zoey's cancer has ruined this storyline. The plot has changed, with Zoey abdicating her role all too soon, and me left reading the full script on my own. My feelings of loss, of the emptiness of an uninhabited home, the missing, the silence in my house, my wishes for a partner to share my thoughts and feelings, my sorrow at having no one to tell my mundane daily news – these stand freshly before me, as if I'd pulled a Band-Aid off a wound. I have no compunctions about talking to my dog; Zoey would have heard all of these personal trials, these minor griefs, and on some level she would have understood. For my part, I would have had a fellow being with whom to share the contents of my heart. I am, instead, facing the prospect of aloneness.

As a member of a species that lives in packs, Zoey's natural inclination is to seek out company. When we're in the house, she settles nearby. She sleeps in our bedrooms, preferably in our beds. She relocates with us as we move around the house. She grapples with massive stress when we are outside, working in the yard or getting the mail, and she is left inside. She whines and pines when we prepare

to leave her, fueling her anxiety with the obvious signals
– shoes being donned, jackets being zipped, a purse being
slung over a shoulder. You might say, in fact, that this
dog is more human than we are in expressing, openly and
unapologetically, her need for human company.

This need for companionship seems qualitatively
different from the need for an intimate partner's love,
for a *relationship*. In my twenties, surrounded by friends
and other companions, I keenly experienced the urge for
relationship. Like probably most young adults, I obsessed
about finding the right partner, and rode a roller coaster
of crushes and doldrums, self-transcending hopes and self-
deprecating despair.

For all my inner turmoil surrounding the elusive
Relationship, my outer life remained remarkably devoid
of action. While to others I may have appeared a loner, to
myself I was a reject. With marriage, much to my relief,
I put a check in the relationship box. But I still longed
for a sense of intimacy and connection. An unabashed
traditionalist, I never considered the option of seeking these
qualities through outside relationships, while married;
intimacy was to come from one place only. When I finally
admitted the lack of love in my marriage, and even more
finally managed to find the nerve to act on this knowledge,
I pulled out. Lack of a husband translated into greater
room for simple companionship, for the support of friends
and other acquaintances. For a time, these sufficed; the
first couple years post-divorce saw me lacking the burning
desire, the energy, and the will to seek out intimacy.

This desert of the newly divorced gave way to a few dating years, a spread of four years or so of searching and introducing, visions awakened and quickly dismissed, as I tried meeting men through singles events, the Internet, the personals. I managed a succession of short-lived relationships, each one teaching me valuable lessons about myself. I was, it seemed, in a bizarre sort of school, amassing lessons in a cumulative way toward, hopefully, greater understanding. My enrollment was voluntary, motivated by desire for that elusive one, the partner.

It is hard to maintain momentum with dating; this activity, at least on a prolonged timeline, is for twenty-somethings, whose propensity for drama also arms them with stamina. Those of us who have come to appreciate calm are challenged to keep up the effort. We go through phases of energized excitement followed by the crash, which is essentially burn-out applied on the relationship front, usually accompanied by heightened despair. Two years ago, I gave up my subscriptions to the internet sites and opted out of the search. Will I return? Undoubtedly. When? I honestly have no idea. The hiatus, however, allows me time to integrate what my experiences, what I've learned, my observations. To reflect.

For one thing, I now realize (fully, in an internalized way) that approaching dating from a position of need, however slight, is folly. Neediness can only attract neediness; this is hardly the basis for a strong relationship which, by definition, brings together individuals, each complete in his or her self, who want to enjoy, appreciate, and support one another.

And then, there is the issue of locus. Where is love? Is it always just beyond reach, in someone else's grasp but not our own? With love, so many of us are on a heroic journey, a quest for the Holy Grail. We search, destined not to find it because of the fatal flaw in our logic, our dooming myopia. For while engaged in a search for love *outside* of ourselves, we're bound to walk right past it, to miss finding it at its source – inside our own hearts. In this sense, I don't regret, for a minute, the two-plus years of downtime I've spent getting to know, and to love, my self better. If I ever find myself in another relationship, I'll be in a much better position to create a healthy, loving, strong, and enduring partnership, one that allows both of us (me and…?) to grow and bloom into our best selves.

And if I never do find that person, well, I have still found the Holy Grail, the source of love, and will have a loving relationship as the core of my life. Never mind that the relationship is with myself, or rather, my Self, that higher aspect of me that communes with God. Ultimately, it's that central relationship with ourselves that will lead us further in the quest, to our true source – to Love, Spirit, if you will, God.

Yes, it's nice to have companionship. I, for one, still hope for that (and from a human). I'll miss Zoey's company so terribly, it is, at this point, beyond imagining. But I also know that I can turn to my self for the love I need, and that I can find within me the Love, the God, that makes all love possible. Lonely, yes. Maybe even painfully so. But I know that neither I, nor anyone else, will ever be truly alone.

18

A dog like Zoey makes an easy travel companion. Like a gypsy, colorful and free-spirited, she's always eager to go. Where? It doesn't matter. The open road, or path, or sidewalk even, beckons enticingly. She's enthusiastic, energized, loving every new sight, sound and, especially, smell. At a trim 25 pounds, she's totally portable. And she travels light.

In this last realm, my dog puts humans to shame. As infants, we can't go anywhere without bags of stuff, covering a spectrum of anticipated needs ranging from food (bottle or sippy cup) to entertainment (squishy toy) to hygiene (diaper and wipes). As children, we are saddled with backpacks that carry our lunch, school assignments, athletic paraphernalia, extra clothing just in case, technological gadgets, increasingly.

As adults, after undergoing decades of growth and supposed maturation, we still haven't acquired much restraint. We travel long distances encumbered by suitcases, carry-ons, day bags, cosmetic cases, computers, and assorted electronics in their respective coverings. Nearer to home, we take purses or backpacks, sometimes a book or magazine, sunglasses. I know many people who carry a comb and/or toothbrush at all times, an admirable habit to be sure, but also a testimony to the burden of preparedness.

As a college student, I was fortunate to matriculate with a slew of college course equivalents under my belt, that is, I had enough credits for Advanced Placement exams and such to allow me a "free" year of college credit. What did I do with this time? Travel.

Barely turned nineteen, young and starry-eyed, and a freshman, I had visions of seeing the world. In chinks of time between classes, I typed letters to the tourist bureaus of countries across Europe, Asia, and the Middle East, requesting travel brochures and maps. (In 1979, there was no internet.) I worked campus food service jobs, to save money. I planned avidly, decided upon must-see destinations, daydreamed about exotic cultures and scenarios, calculated my daily budget, explored various traveling scenarios and logistics, voraciously fantasizing and accumulating visions.

In these visions, mobility was a central feature of me and my traveling lifestyle. I anchored my months abroad with a few lengthy stops: an initial two-month stay on an Israeli moshav, where I spent an excruciating ten hours per day on my knees in the desert, picking gargantuan sweet red peppers; a two-week stay at Taize, a monastery in rural eastern France, where I spent time in total silence, learning to quiet both outer and inner voices; a visit to Findhorn, the collective farm in northern Scotland renowned for growing thirty-pound cabbages and other vegetable monstrosities, with the help of mystical powers. But apart from these respites, for many months I changed location nearly every two or three days. If I wanted to maintain my freedom of motion, a suitcase was out of the question.

Instead, for months on end, I lived out of a backpack. Not the sort they sell for actual backpacking, one of those large sporty varieties with a frame, side pouches, hip belt, and numerous cleverly placed compartments, preferably with zipper closure. No, this was more of a knapsack, a student-sized pack, but even less elaborate than those used today by most school kids for their books, homework, and lunch. Mine fit three pairs of underwear, one change of clothes, a washcloth (which performed double-duty as my towel), bar of soap, comb, toothbrush, and the critical documents: passport, traveler's checks which I cashed and doled out to myself in $8 per day increments, and Eurail pass. This was traveling at its leanest.

I quickly found how little I need. Yes, I wore the same clothes every other day, but who cares? Knowing I'd never see any of my new acquaintances again, I threw concern for appearances out the window. They could think what they want to think, only to take their impressions away with them on the next train. Mirrors, that bane of the modern-day woman's existence, lost their power over me – at first, on the moshav and through Greece, because there weren't any; and by the time I reached the more civilized hostels of Europe, where extravagances such as mirrors were to be found in communal bunk rooms, because I had ceased to gauge my day by how I was looking. Lack of options made choices about appearance – for instance, what to wear – pleasantly simple (Option 1, or Option 2); as such, they ceased to commandeer any of my mind's time or energy. On the personal maintenance front, my activities devolved into the barest of basics: brushing my teeth, and washing with soap and water. Imagine that! The processes involved in packing up and leaving one hostel, and arriving in another, in aggregate took a minute, at most. I had achieved nearly dog-level portability.

The benefits of my newfound mobility were profound – a sense of freedom, of unburdening, of simplicity. The logistical advantages were apparent on a daily basis, as I watched other travelers (usually Americans) lugging oversized backpacks and suitcases on and off trains, to and from hostels or pensions. How burdensome their loads; and correspondingly, how burdened their lives, even while traveling! My freedom, by contrast, was delicious.

As my travels wore on, another interesting aspect of the unburdening dawned on me: I met people easily. In the off-season, that is, winter/spring and other times not coinciding with the college vacations of American students on semesters abroad, my fellow youth hostelers came predominantly from Germany and Australia, with a smattering of Canadians, Scandinavians, Brits, and others.

Traveling solo, I settled into a companion-seeking routine whereby, on arriving at the train station in a new city or town, I immediately walked to the youth hostel. First things first: I checked in for the night and chose my bunk. Immediately after, I scanned the common rooms for compatible and socially available travelers. Age and gender rated lower on my scale of eligibility criteria than did general friendliness. Identifying a possible co-traveler, I then approached the person(s) to ask a few ice-breaking questions, which led more often than not to a companionship spent covering the local streets, museums, markets, squares, parks, and churches. We would pass 24 hours as new friends and co-travelers, for usually a couple of days and spanning meals, exploration of the city or local environs, and ongoing talk, conversations that covered everything from family history to politics, art, travels, and goals and visions for the future, ending with, of course, night-time at the hostel. Sometimes I traveled onward to a next destination in the company of such a friend, but more often, alone.

I'd always been shy, introverted in the sense of needing time and space to myself, so it came as a surprise that this repeated meeting and friendship, meeting and friendship, along with the uninterrupted togetherness with strangers, flowed so easily. Until, one day, a German friend, in perfect English and an also perfect (to my ears) German accent, pointed out the obvious, "You're not like all the other Americans. You can always tell the Americans because they travel in twos and threes. You're the only one by yourself." I had inadvertently hit upon another layer of unburdening – a stripping away not only of one's possessions, of extraneous stuff, but also of our protective social layer, in this case, of surrounding one's self with fellow Americans, with people like me. Without that peculiar sort of armor, I became disarmed myself and, to these strangers in foreign lands, entirely open.

In the context of our modern lives, the feasibility of stripping down presents a bit of an issue. We can feng shui our living areas, declutter our kitchen cabinets, donate our unwanted blazers and bookshelves to Goodwill. This, to be sure, is all positive. It's good for the planet, and good for our mental, psychological, and physical health. Clutter, in fact, has risen in prominence; magazines rail against it, coaches assist us in excising it from our houses and homes, spiritual materialists offer any number of programs to cleanse our bodies and minds of its persistent sullying presence. Economic advisers and environmentalists join hands in encouraging us to pare away all nonessentials, purchase frugally, reduce and reuse. There is an irony in these injunctions, arising from the midst of the most consumerist society on the face of the earth.

My forty-second birthday was destined to be nothing special. I was home, going through the usual motions, maintaining house, yard, and family, toggling between roles as camp chauffeur and proposal writer, swimming in the early hours and walking the dog at the other end of the day, making an unrelenting stream of lunches and dinners. A welcome break came in the form of an invitation from a fellow swimmer and friend to a birthday lunch. "Let me cook for you. You will be my guest," she had promised, ceremoniously. Salmon was mentioned as a strong possibility. Together with this immediate (fish) hook, came the prospect of some girlfriend time, and both appealed to me immensely. Ah, a real birthday! Leanne had just moved to a new house, so I was eager to see this, as well.

Let me provide just a little background on Leanne. She is recently divorced, independently wealthy, not working nor ever having needed to do so. She is a free bird, her two sons having recently graduated from college and moved to far corners of the country. Active and athletic, she is always on the go, engaged in all manner of intellectual and cultural, as well as physical events. She is a paragon of energy, and of privilege.

Our lunch date was scheduled for noon, but pulling away from my work on that day proved a bit harder than anticipated. I phoned Leanne to say that I would be about twenty minutes late. Arriving on that amended timeline, she presented me with a plate of brown rice and carrots, very healthy, I was assured. The salmon, I was told, had been bought in small portion, just enough for the two of us — so as not to have any waste. Because it was getting cold, and could not have been much good, she ate it. I was crestfallen. What had been offered as an act of generosity, and presented as a treat, had turned into the antithesis —

a statement of unworthiness (for salmon, yes, but more importantly, for special care).

There is a power in the giving and receiving of Special Things – often those things that cost us dearly, either in money, time, energy, or other personal resources – that carries a strong message of deservingness, of being valued. This message is a good one, not bad, and one we can allow as an act of kindness to ourselves and others.

As I was eating my downgraded birthday lunch, Leanne made use of the time to package up some return merchandise, using cardboard box, brown tape, and marker. She was sending back to L.L. Bean, a company with (in those days) a lifetime return policy, a well-worn, eight-year-old backpack on which the zipper had broken.

While I wholly agree with, and adhere to, many aspects of simple living in its various guises, not the least of which is environmental, I'm repelled at the same time by its inherent stinginess. Life is bountiful, beautiful, replete with wonders. We are so fortunate to be alive, and to live in a time and place in which many of us have all that we need and want, and so much more. Gratitude, not stinginess, is in order. Can we allow the free flow of plenty, of pleasures, but do so in a responsible way, stopping short of excess? Can we be generous with ourselves and each other, in a way that helps but does no harm?

The take-home lesson of my travels still asserts itself – generosity, and a sense of abundance, has much more to do with the cultivation of an unencumbered, accepting, open spirit than with the presence of anything external, whether things or money or even other people. Giving can be done in many ways, concrete and intangible. And less, it turns out, really can be more.

In the realm of food, detail has always eluded Zoey. Suppertime, or breakfast for that matter, is a two- or three-minute affair. She mostly avoids chewing; it slows her down. Instead, she takes in her food in ravenous gulps, noisily, with great commotion and full focus.

My kids, by contrast, have learned to discriminate. The original Oreos, in their blue, black, and white packaging, are infinitely preferable to lower-cost imitations. "Chocolate sandwich cookies" from known manufacturers (Keebler, perhaps, or Healthy Choice) don't stand a chance, and store-brand "sandwich creams"? Forget it. Pepperidge Farm goldfish beat out generic copies, hands down. Cheerios, in their original incarnation, have a huge edge over the multiple other "o's" – toastie-o's, tastie-o's, happy-o's, you name it.

While my kids good-naturedly consume the tofu mixtures I concoct, maintaining an open mind to the world of wholesome and organic edibles, the discriminating powers of their palates emerge in response to product differentiation, to those items for which marketers have created a niche, promoting them to carefully targeted consumers. The food advertising industry teaches unaware youth and adults alike to be experts, fine-tuned to the specific merits of its products. Contrast this product-ification of so-called foods to, say, the treatment of real food, broccoli for instance, which, without marketing, remains for the most part simply broccoli.

Fortunately, neither marketers nor peers have sole power over our tastes. As I experiment with cooking different items – shall I put shitake or portobello mushrooms in my scrambled eggs this morning? – I find my own culinary life taking on subtler hues and finer gradations. I consider the relative merits of leeks versus shallots, in preparing a pureed cauliflower soup. I mix herbs with differing characters to give dishes depth and aroma, a sprinkling of red pepper flakes to add zing, basil for a hearty base of flavor, a splash of orange juice to balance the pungent tones of cayenne. I may be approaching the level of differentiation that Zoey enjoys through her sense of smell, if not taste. As I elevate the value of the details, exquisiteness slowly and cautiously shows its face.

I was married to a man who had never learned to play piano. Early in our relationship, I underestimated the significance of this historical fact. After all, this was dimly lit history, and he had made a start. His mother had taken him to almost a year's worth of private piano lessons, before capitulating to a first grader's resistance. From that brief introduction to musical training, he retained nothing; he has never been able to read music, never proceeded to study music theory, never had the experience of playing a Mozart sonata, being part of a chamber ensemble, joining his music to others' in a junior orchestra.

My parents, on the other hand, raised four children on piano lessons, a weekly ritual extending from first grade through high school. Music instruction was a given, an unquestioned part of one's education, on a par with any basic life skill such as braiding one's hair or riding a bike. Why, you may wonder, should this difference in childhood backgrounds matter one iota in the course of an adult relationship? Beyond the obvious classism, with the red flags it raises when young twenty-somethings from different backgrounds join paths, there's the issue of detail.

Said husband had missed an epigenetic window, a golden opportunity to switch on a vital gene, namely, the one that enables the bearer to appreciate classical music. Like ducklings that can only imprint to follow the mother duck during a brief and finite developmental period, he had passed through the classical music imprinting phase without the proper inputs; once having exiting that phase, he lost his ability to enjoy the wide world of fine music. To him, a Chopin etude and a Tchaikovsky symphony were indistinguishable, falling equally into a bucket labeled "classical." Synonymous with boring. With this cursory dismissal, a summative judgment, he deprived himself of access to vast horizons of enjoyment, to discernment in the dimension of hearing.

Proposing what he saw as a viable alternative, he introduced me to heavy metal.

Discernment cuts across all axes of our lives. Taste, sound, smell. Our best developed sense, our sight, gives us incredible capacity to appreciate detail and dimension. Just think of the variety of flowers in our world, the innumerable colors, shapes, sizes, textures, stages of unfolding, bloom, and wither. With flowers, the link between attention to specifics, to unique qualities, on the one hand, and to the sensation of beauty on the other, is very clear. It's no less present, though, when we take in a full array of information from our other senses; we can access beauty through appreciation of unique loveliness in any realm.

A young child looks at a rose and sees, "flower." She looks at a lily, and again sees, "flower." Same for clover or crocus, dahlia or verbena. Over the course of growing up, she increasingly learns to differentiate and then, hopefully, to appreciate flowers in an expanded and amplified way as well. She know dozens, maybe hundreds, of types of flower loveliness, not just one.

Education, at its best, nudges us along in a similar process, the increasing sophistication of perception. We learn to differentiate matter in various ways – as chemicals, atoms and molecules, categories of plant, geologic forms. We learn to differentiate language into its structure, cadence, flow, syntax, sound and rhythm. We learn to differentiate the factors affecting personality structure in psychology, the forces propelling the actions of societies in economics and sociology, the personages and ideologies that chart the course of humanity through politics and history.

How do we assess an education? Perhaps we should consider the extent to which it enables us to appreciate a vastness of experience, to find beauty in the kaleidoscopic array of detail and difference. And on at even more general level, to value difference itself as not threatening and problematic, something to be "resolved," but as a source of richness, texture, beauty, growth. For the truth is, we forget much of the specific information we drill into our minds over the course of our school years, and even most of the knowledge which we accumulate along the highways and byways of our adult lives. But the capacity to appreciate the detail, to discern the exquisite uniqueness of whatever we encounter, will continue to allow us access to beauty, and from there, to a love of life and a fulfillment within it.

20

"Zoooo-eeey, you're scaring me with that thing on your shoulder," Carolyn's friend whined, hanging back rather than bursting through the front door. In conspicuous departure from her usual greeting, she decided not to give our pup the customary pat on the head. Erin has had a long-standing fondness for Zoey. Her typical, exuberant entrance includes a boisterous, musical, "Zoey!! Hello Puh-deee!" Now she shrinks back, withholding her affection out of fear.

Most weekday mornings, I swim at the Chapel Hill Community Center's public pool. I arrive at 5:25 a.m. sharp, at the same time as a woman who is almost an institution around our town, Carla. She is easily recognizable. The victim of bone cancer at age sixteen, she lost her left leg in her doctors' efforts to save her young life. Nearly forty years later, she is fit, athletic, well-loved, and well-known in the local scene. I once overheard her describing how she handled people who felt uncomfortable around her disability. "I feel sort of sorry for them, actually," she began, "it's like they don't know what to do, whether it's OK to look or not. They don't know if they should say anything." Adults, with our uncertainties about what is appropriate, acceptable, or kind, have a harder time with the unusual than do younger people. "Children are easier," Carla elaborated, "They just blurt things out. Then their mothers come along and try to hush them up, feeling all awkward about it like their kids have done something wrong."

Our avoidance of physical difference, especially "deformity," has deep roots in fear. For Zoey, fear of the physically unknown is straightforward; after all, something unknown can be dangerous. Best to protect yourself, to bark.

When we humans face physical issues in another human, we grapple with a complex mix of uncertainties: we don't want to hurt the other's feelings, we worry about making him or her feel scrutinized, judged as inferior, deficient, separate, or even just simply unlike the rest of us. When we face disease or disability in an animal, our fear arises from a more basic instinct, one that is less emotionally modulated, more directly existential. We don't like to admit the possibility that the body, whether belonging to an animal or a person, can let us down. Bodies, it turns out, can grow in bizarre ways; they can deteriorate, break, or give out on us; they can lose parts; they can malfunction.

All of this, marked by our brains as wrong, disturbing, even grotesque (think of a dog hopping along on three legs, the result of being hit by a car), scares us.

"Erin…" I coaxed her. "What Zoey needs from you at this point is as much love as you can give her. She won't understand why she grosses you out, all she'll feel is that you're not patting her and loving her the way you used to." Erin softened, and gave Zo-Zo a tentative pat, then a few long caressing strokes. "She needs all of us now to be as kind to her as we can." "Poor Puddy," Erin crooned.

Like cut glass that reflects light at different angles, fear has multiple facets that strike us in different ways, eliciting differing reactions. My fear of Zoey's pain, or of seeing her suffer, my fear of facing her loss of physical capacities, doesn't cause repulsion; on the contrary, it draws me closer. I want to hold her closer than close, to shield her from these forces of physical erosion, to protect her from having to advance into a fearsome unknown, the future. And if she must go that route, I am overcome by the urge, almost desperate in its impossibility, to save her from traveling that path alone.

This morning, I took Zoey with me on a walk around the golf course of the Washington Duke Inn. The five-kilometer loop doubles as the Duke cross-country course for college athletes, and as the Duke Fitness Trail for university faculty, students, or locals looking for a pleasant wooded walk. On any given day, at any given time, the trail is being traversed by a parade of dogs– good-natured golden retrievers, mutts of all sorts, lean and athletic boxers, feisty little terriers. Zoey has trodden its well-worn track dozens, maybe hundreds, of times, each time making new friends among dogs and their human companions. Ordinarily, our arrival in the gravel parking lot, and our setting foot and paw, respectively, upon the six-foot-wide dirt swath that forms a 45-minute circuit, is an occasion for great excitement. Zoey, typically, rejoices.

Today, she lagged. The weather was chilly, not even reaching the freezing point on our car thermometer. As we headed down the first slope, she stopped frequently to sniff, dawdled, limped, and when I looked behind me to check in on her, she cast me forlorn glances. Ten minutes further along, a congenial elderly jogger in a Duke sweatshirt commented, "it looks like your partner's not so sure about this." In truth, I had deliberated the pros and cons of bringing her on this excursion, and had finally conceded to my son's view. Sam felt that Zoey would be happier walking with me than being left at home alone. Part-way into the walk, I realized the fundamental flaw in his logic – had she felt well, she would certainly have been happier walking, but…

Zoey stayed a full leash-length behind me for most of the walk. A gap of sorrow, measured in blue nylon web, separated us as I realized that this might well be her last voyage around the Fitness Trail, and my last time enjoying her company on this familiar walk. Her pleasure in the event had vanished. Instead, she dutifully trudged behind me, only joining me to trot side by side when she knew we were nearing our car.

My sadness is immense, tinged with fear as the course of her days becomes clearer. Hope is giving way, being dragged down by the gravity of an increasingly visible future. There are still many uncertainties, true, and they all entail some aspect of fear. Will she suffer? Will I know how to help her, what to do, how to be with her? Will I be able to help my children through this crisis, or will I be too much engulfed in my own grief? And ultimately, how will I ever live with this loss?

I am afraid for Zoey, for myself, for my children, not knowing if and how we will handle the pain, the grief, and the emptiness following the unthinkable, the unfathomable, end of Zoey. (How can a *being* have an end? This is beyond grasping.)

Yet I know that my fear, unlike repulsion at a physical abnormality, grows out of a deep love. It holds within it the seeds of growth, inner strength, and re-appreciation of life. It may lead me to a re-investment in the living, those all around me and even myself. If we could only see – and accept – these gains in advance, we might suffer less as we endure the process of loss.

21

Zoey has been such a good sport about her illness and its effects. No complaints, no whining. As the tumor grows, she becomes slower, more tentative in her movements, less perky and energetic. But she never grumbles or protests. She is, you might say, a paragon of acceptance.

That said, she's been understandably reluctant to relinquish some of her capacities, particularly when they support her familiar patterns and comforts. As I type away at these pages, sitting at a flimsy corner workstation made of particle board masquerading as white maple, Zoey likes to keep me company. She jumps onto a dark purple chair we've moved next to the computer and settles herself onto the seat cushion, leaning back against a soft, lavender, chenille pillow we've added for her. In her distinctive way, through her presence, she's helping me with my work – and I appreciate her support.

In recent days, however, she's hesitated a bit before jumping up into her purple chair; rather than spryly, unwaveringly, springing up, she has rocked back and forth on all fours, given a few test lurches, then hopped up, rather unsteadily. Once she didn't quite make it, a poignant failure. Shortly thereafter, she gave up, in silent recognition of her mounting limitation. Without apology or explanation, she now stands in front of the chair, turns her head in my direction, and looks up at me, her eyes posing a simple, unapologetic request for help. I tenderly lift her and settle her in, planting a kiss on her furry forehead as I do.

Zoey's "business" has followed a similar downward spiral. She has progressed from jogging around the block to walking the same circuit, then walking out to our yard, then being carried out. The transition at each stage has pained me, each cutback forcing on me the information that she's no longer capable of the status quo.

Zoey has taken it all in stride. Given the choice, of course, she would leap at the opportunity to move freely, joyously, unencumbered, youthfully. But instead, keeping step with her circumstances, she progressively limits herself. She does maintain some drive, an encouraging sort of effort. For example, while she requires me to retrieve her from the couch, where she's begun to spend most of her daytime hours, or from her doggie bed, and to pick her up and carry her outdoors, she still insists on tottering back indoors using her own four legs – a sight that sends pangs, like darts of sorrow, through my heart.

And then came a day when she finished her business, hobbled a few steps across the grass, stopped, and turned to look up at me. Please, her eyes said, help me. More than just bruised, my heart bled as I picked up her small sweet frame, hugged her close, and brought her back in to her couch. Clinging to the stability of her normal schedule, I prepared her meal: at this point, it was a mush consisting of organic ground beef, softened soy protein, olive oil, organic whole milk, and numerous supplements. I attempted to spoon-feed her as she lay on the couch cushion, conscious that I'm grasping at straws, willing to try anything that offers the hope of wellness.

Does Zoey concern herself with all the trouble she's putting me through? Not at all. Would I want her to? Simply, no.

In my junior year of college, one of my six roommates imparted the secret to her stunning popularity. I had not yet met Maria when I arrived on campus after many months of travel. Roommate selection and the housing lottery had taken place during the second semester of my sophomore year, while I was off traveling through the Middle East and Europe. I had been, almost literally, in a different world, one where details such as college dormitories seemed a far-fetched concept.

My friends back on the home front, fortunately, had remained firmly ensconced in this reality. They had somehow orchestrated a coup: in the campus housing lottery, they had won claim to the seven-person suite that occupied the top floor of Blair Tower – a landmark, the university's centrally located clock tower. The tower rises above a majestic arch, constructed in academic gothic style, under which hundreds, maybe a thousand, students pass each day. It is tall. With twelve flights of stairs between ground level and the door to our suite, my roommates and I could forego Stairmaster for the duration.

A bit disoriented after my time away, I showed up a bit late on move-in day, in the warm but pleasant air of early September in New Jersey. Five of my roommates had already begun settling in, but I hesitated. I searched for familiar faces, then avoided the scene by roaming the lovely campus, revisiting a few familiar sites, appreciating its beauty. Eventually I considered the daunting prospect of moving my boxes, which had been stored in the basement of another dormitory, an imposing brownstone, up into daylight, across a couple courtyards, and then up an infinity of stairs. We were about to live, after all, in a tower, the stuff of fairytales. (Rapunzel, here we come.)

Never one to ask for help, I started in with the first box, a cardboard carton taped shut and filled with who-knows-what. Something, I assumed, that would be useful to my college student self, or I wouldn't have bothered storing it. Heading into a brief stint as Pack Animal Ascending With Load (and returning, reloading, reascending), I noticed something odd. A team of three or four students, exuding maleness, looking fit, athletic, and willing, were trekking up and down the tower's numberless flights of stairs. Time and again. In good spirits, fresh and bounding with energy. Now this tower had no other floors than the top one, and no other rooms at its top than ours. The only possible conclusion was that these guys were carrying boxes, furniture, lamps, even a dorm-sized refrigerator to our all-girls' suite. Interesting.

And then I met Maria, charming, beautiful, southern, warm, engaging Maria. One of my roommates.

These guys, it turned out, had agreed – voluntarily – to move Maria's possessions, which were considerable, from sea level to tower altitude, for no other reason than for her. Cool and not the least bit sheepish, smiling, Maria stood by and presided over their efforts. I was amazed. Where, after all, was her fear of imposing? How would she ever be able to reciprocate? Wasn't she digging herself into a hole of indebtedness? As two strapping young men, who might have been heading afterward to the rugby team meeting, lifted her refrigerator and began the climb, I couldn't resist asking. Who are these guys? And *how* did you get them to do this? Her answer, delivered with a genuinely friendly gaze, stopped me in my tracks. "I [pronounced, 'ah'] asked."

Maria's genteel Southern mother, a bastion of Charleston society, had taught her certain truths that I, with my frugal, discrete, rugged, Yankee roots, had missed. Maria had learned as a little girl that, if you want to make friends, you have to ask them to do things for you. You request favors. This comes in stark contrast to my upbringing, the lesson there having been one of self-reliance, of doing for one's self, and at all costs, not imposing on others; and the corollary being that one should always "do unto others," preferably without thought for one's self. I was raised on a one-sided version of the Golden Rule, on the notion that it is "more blessed to give than to receive," and given my desire to overcome my selfish nature, I interpreted this to mean that giving should be the sole focus. I practiced self-effacement as if it were a pass to, if not virtue, at least being liked.

Applying her Southern wisdom in the college scene, Maria amassed a considerable fan club (read, men) by *allowing* them to help her, by asking and then graciously receiving. The concept of Incurring burden, or worse yet exhibiting entitlement, simply did not factor into the equation.

An interesting side effect of Maria's favor-asking strategy became quickly apparent. She was attractive. I am not talking just about looks; she had a charisma that, I deduced, had something to do with the appeal of asking, of inviting others to help and letting them do so. Her allure extended not only to guys, many of whom adored and/or idolized her, but to other college girls as well. A sort of magnetism, of charm, resulted from the currents of self-assurance, self-possession, and self-worth. Very little doubt showed through, nor did any discernible anxiety about what others would think. She asked, she received, and in the receiving she actually made friends, rather than losing, alienating, or offending them. Imagine that!

Zoey didn't show any pain until Saturday, March 11, two full months after her diagnosis. My kids were at their dad's house, where they spent alternate weekends. I had made myself a peaceful dinner, eaten sitting on the floor next to Zoey, who was resting in her doggie bed, taken her out in my arms for an early evening visit with nature, then gone through my bath and assorted bedtime ablutions. Zoey was curled up in a corner of my bedroom, where she's been sleeping for the past few weeks. Emerging from the bathroom, I was greeted by a whimper. And then she began to cry. Not to whine, nor whimper; this was crying, and she didn't stop. I talked to her, patted her, soothed her, explained, questioned, reassured, pleaded. I sang her lullabies, tears streaming down my face. And still she cried. By 9:00 p.m., I was beside myself. My dog was, undeniably, in pain.

Desperate for help, but uncertain what to do, I phoned my neighbor, a consummate cat-lover who has rescued countless stray felines. Kim's heart is far softer than average, arguably a defect as it causes her to adopt troubled cats with abandon. Word seems to travel in the cat world, which provides for Kim with a steady supply of its members in need. She's had, at various times, up to eight cats in the modestly sized house which she, her husband, and her son also occupy. The litter box detail, at those times, becomes a monumental job. For me, pinch hitting briefly when the family is on vacation, it is yeoman's duty; for Kim, it's a daily act of service.

And so, in my distress, I called Kim to obtain the phone number of the local after-hours veterinary emergency hospital. I received the receptionist, choked out my story, and told her to expect us in thirty minutes. Kim had offered for her thirteen-year-old son, Michael, an equally big-hearted being, to go with me; I had declined, not wanting to have to protect a kid, as well as my pup, from pain, or to put on a cheery or brave face. Given the state I was in, though, I knew I couldn't drive. What to do? I called my dear friend Mary, who had driven on my last middle-of-night Disaster Run; she had taken my son and me to the far side of Raleigh at two o'clock in the morning, so that he could be admitted to the only psychiatric hospital in the region with a free bed. No one answered at Mary and Tom's house, but I sobbed an incoherent SOS into their answering machine, nonetheless. I hung up, and the phone rang. "Jane?" Kim began, "Do you want me to drive you?" Kim is a nurse; she had to go to work the next morning, despite the fact that it would be Sunday. I knew that she would set her alarm at 5:30 a.m., would be in her car and heading out of her driveway no later than 6:30. She couldn't have scripted a more welcome message. "Yes" was all I managed to blurt out. After all, if I drove, who would hold Zoey?

And so, Kim and I took Zoey to the veterinary emergency room, waited for hours (ironically, pets and humans alike have to wait the longest at the times that are most urgent), discussed her situation with a kind vet assigned to night shift, and came home with a prescription pain medication, with an initial dose already on its way through pup's system. Zoey calmed down in my arms during the ride home, and seemed to be nodding off as we pulled into the driveway.

We returned to a surprising scene: My entire house was brightly lit, even the garage light was on, and two sets of headlights flooded the driveway. My bleary, weary, distraught mind struggled for a moment to make sense of this brightness, this scene. And then I saw Mary. "Where were you??!" Unable to make out my message, my friend had driven to every emergency room within a twenty-mile radius. At 10:00 p.m., 11:00 p.m., 12:00 midnight. While Kim and I had waited in the pet emergency room for hours, Mary had criss-crossed town on local streets, had zipped along the highway from our town to two neighboring cities, unsure what disaster had befallen me, imagining that it again involved Sam. Tom had come down to case out our house, search for clues as to what had happened, and figure out their next steps.

I gingerly emerged from Kim's car, with Zoey in my arms. What had I put my friends through?! I was, and still am, overcome by gratitude for their kindness and concern. After a mortified – but fleeting – realization of what I'd inflicted on them, I let go of the well-ingrained commandment, *Thou shalt not impose*. Instead, I accepted ever so gratefully what they had given me – compassion, support, love.

When scoping out the scene of our hasty middle-of-night departure, mine and Zoey's, Tom had noticed something. He had used their key to my house to enter via the front door, then headed out through the garage door to see if my car was there. A clue: it was. This puzzled him. How could I have left without my car? And at this hour, why? Where could I have gone without it?

Meanwhile, he made a mental note that the door from house to garage was missing its doorknob. The thing had jammed, then broken, a few months ago. Given its scale of importance, and the number of household tasks ahead of it in queue, this item had taken a number and been seated. Sam had removed the dysfunctional hardware, leaving a straightforward round hole in the wood. To block the cold winter air from streaming into the house, I stuffed the hole with an old pair of panty hose (a commodity in no short supply, given my job in Development).

A good handyman and meticulous in keeping up his own home, Tom had been unimpressed by my solution to the doorknob quandary. "If you have anything that needs fixing, *just call,*" he enjoined, after we explained the evening's history. Kim seconded this with an offer to send Ken, her master mechanic of a husband, over to help as well.

Have I done so? In these small matters, the fear of imposition still looms large. My panty hose, standing guard in lieu of a doorknob, continues to form a barrier between the outside air of the garage and inside warmth of our house. No, I haven't asked for help. But then, this doorknob is a small matter. What's more important is my certainty, now based on solid evidence, that I have friends on whom I can call, without imposing, for the real needs.

For Zoey, I'll buy any remedy or prepare any potion, carry her outside or lift her onto her chair whenever she asks, and cater to her every need, even those I know only exist in my desperate imaginings. My mind struggles to *find* ways to help. And yet none of this makes me feel imposed upon. No, she does not impose on me. I love her, and love wastes none of its precious attention on such a trivial concept.

22

Zoey once got me into trouble, big trouble, with my neighbors, the couple whose driveway directly faces mine, whose house is a stone's throw away from own home. At the time, Zoey was a mere puppy, partially trained, still vulnerable, lacking street-smarts, and above all, impulsive. I was a beleaguered stay-at-home mom and wife, volunteering in my children's classrooms at the Montessori preschool and public elementary school, dashing here and there on endless errands of house and family, exhausting myself in trying to maintain the perfect home. And to be a perfect neighbor.

We had moved into our small neighborhood a few years ago, as the first owners of our home, a mid-sized house in a new, and still partially constructed, development counting some two dozen homes. Our various neighbors, like us, were young families who had recently purchased their houses; many of them, too, were first-time homeowners with young children. For me, the mom of a toddler and a preschooler, the situation was ideal. Our neighborhood cul-de-sac became a group playspace in the afternoons, mothers casually talking while watching their children, interfering now and then to smooth out a squabble or comment on a less-than-model behavior. We had children ranging in age from infant, in front pack or stroller, to kindergartener, on foot or tricycle; one boy, Ethan, the oldest and a precocious athlete even at age five, rode a bike.

Ethan knew that he had the edge in this group by virtue of age, size, and coordination, among other things; he kept to himself for the most part. His parents, whom he called by first name, encouraged his "uniqueness" and self-expression. One day that self-expression took the form of full-volume, potty-mouthed, ditties, repeated at lung's capacity over and over as he circled the cul-de-sac on his real bike. With my four-year-old son watching in awe, I was none too pleased with this display of behavior. I made a tactical error, however, in asking him to stop. Another time, I saw him whacking the little fruit tree I'd just planted, with a stick almost as large as the sapling's trunk. Now I take a very protective nurturing stance toward my plants, and therefore jumped instantly to act in this situation. "Ethan, *please don't do that.*" Another time, I saw him poking a stick up and down, up and down, in the drain by the side of our street. What's Ethan doing? I asked another of the neighbor kids. "Yammy's down there," she explained. Yammy, our cat.

After the incident in the cul-de-sac, Ethan's mom, Liz, had spoken to me harshly, in no uncertain terms. I was *not* to speak to her child about his behavior. He's only *five*, she reminded me. She was right, of course. My buttons had been pushed, and I had overstepped. But far from taking this as a simple situation requiring apology, I spiraled into a panicky response. To what – Ethan? the situation in the cul-de-sac? the accusation? No, I was responding to the anger, pure and simple, and my reaction wasn't tinged with any modicum of self-righteousness, any sense that there may have been some understandable reason for my transgression. I was mortified. My inner alarms, finely tuned during childhood, were blaring, drowning out any sensible thoughts. Ah, familiar territory.

True to form, I retreated into my most conciliatory (read, guilty) mode, internally shriveling in fear of Liz, and dedicating myself to meticulous censorship of my own words. Apparently I wasn't very good at this. After committing a couple more faux pas, I scripted in my mind an explanation: Yes, Ethan may be a wonderful human being; Liz, of course, is right. What I object to is his *behavior*, not him. Could she, his mom, please talk with him about this? Not surprisingly, I never summoned up the courage to deliver the request.

One late spring afternoon, I popped four-year-old Carolyn into her car seat and backed the Honda out of the garage. We were running late to pick up Sam from his pottery class, run by Chapel Hill Parks & Recreation, on the other side of town. I had barely pulled out of my driveway, and had just shifted from reverse into first, when Liz came charging across their lawn toward me, walking fast, face grim. I lowered the window. "Jane." She stated, firmly.

There had been a dog-sighting, in their yard. Reportedly a small black-and-white dog. Livid, Liz let loose her fury: she does *not* like dogs, she does *not* want them in her yard, and she most definitely does *not* want them pooping on her grass. And so on.

An eternity, perhaps a minute or two, later, I drove away, shaken, leaving her in the middle of her tirade. I felt bruised, and also indignant. My little, dear, sweet Zoey?! For one thing, I was sure that Zoey had been indoors at the hour of the purported crime.

Anger, one of my earliest challenges, sets me on edge to this day. In my childhood, anger hung over our family as an abiding threat; it lurked in the shadows of our lives, its presence, either overt or thinly hidden, implied the absence of love. When it showed its face, this anger confirmed my unworthiness, powerlessness, and isolation, it whispered to my childish self that most dreaded of messages: I was unwanted.

Like a toxic, stubbornly stable, radioactive substance, a message received in childhood can have a very long half-life. Probably every one of us has some message or other, absorbed early in life, that remains interlaced with our sense of who we are. As adults, we are exquisitely sensitive to new forms of the old message, our responses to it become woven into our behavioral repertoire to help create the fabric of our being. To this day, I avoid angry people and, when I find myself in potentially inflamed situations, I bend over backwards to defuse or evade the confrontation. Conflict avoidance, you might say, is my middle name.

At the time of this last run-in with Liz, Zoey was at most a few months old. She was, admittedly, not exactly a paragon of doggie obedience, and not even entirely under our control. The kids, at ages four and seven, thrilled in the simple victory of opening the electronically operated garage door with the just-within-reach button, and when they did so, Zoey sensed a window of opportunity. She would dash out, simultaneously rebellious and victorious in a particularly puppyish way. Liz's scenario was plausible. But Zoey, the quintessential puppy, was also enormously cute, friendly, endearing, young. Could anyone be angry at a puppy? Well, maybe not, but they could certainly be angry at the puppy's owner.

Peering through tears at the street ahead of me, as I drove with Carolyn to collect Sam from the pottery studio, I made a silent dedication and a promise to myself: I did not *deserve* this treatment. I would *not* put myself in a position to take any more of it. (I later wondered if this lesson was intended as practice for my divorce.)

Meantime, I attempted to understand that, while Liz had triggered my deepest fear, I likely triggered something equally powerful in her. Who knows what? Probably it was none of my business. Maybe I reminded Liz of her mother. There were a myriad of other reasons that I might have irritated her so abrasively, perhaps the reaction was unrelated, or only partially related, to me. Or perhaps this line of thinking just reflected my desire to let myself off the hook. At any rate, the mystery of the "other" remains, and always will. My task is to work on myself, letting the other (a revolving cast of characters) do the same, and maintaining the compassionate sensibility that this work is as hard for him or her as it for me.

More evidence, challenging me to ignore it, emerged a short while later when Liz had a word or two with my painter, concerning the new color of my house. Nate was in the driveway, having only just begun the house painting job. Liz strode up to him. "What do you think of *yellow.*" She began, not exactly asking. "Well, ma'am, I think it's rather nice," said Nate, respectfully, addressing a woman, in his thick drawl. "Well I *don't.*" According to Nate, the language got worse from there. "If she wasn't a woman, I would have told her exactly what I thought of her." Evidently the issue was now no longer the color yellow. "And if you weren't such a nice lady, I would tell you what a …. well, you know, pardon my words, ma'am."

Whatever the cause, whatever my stance as I determined to navigate it with some (however tiny) bit of strength and wisdom, it was horrible to be yelled at – berated like a child – by my neighbor. I quickly formulated a self-protection plan: I would, from here on, be a ghost to the family across the street. I reformulated reality as follows: I could now see them, but they could no longer see me. I could pass in front of them, walking my pup along the sidewalk in front of their house, for instance, and they would look right through me. I was invisible, I could live in plain view, bordering on their lives, but without being watched. I could drop any worries about their judgments because, from now forward, to them I no longer existed.

Almost ten years later, I still, loosely, maintain my neighbor-specific invisibility. They have their lives; I have mine. I see their comings and goings, and I'm sure they see mine. They must have hypothesized about divorce, when my ex-husband's car was no longer parked in the driveway, when he showed up periodically just to whisk the kids away. Have they noticed me carrying Zoey outdoors? That she no longer jogs around the block with me and Sam in the morning? That we are not out on the weekend, in leash and in old running shoes respectively, stopping on the sidewalk to talk with neighborhood friends?

Time has eroded the rawness of emotion; its steady march, too, has brought new circumstances that allow me to make small steps toward reconciliation. Last year, I noticed their daughter's name on the roster for lacrosse, in the same evening session as I'd signed Carolyn up for. It is a ten-minute drive to the lacrosse fields, and the 6:00 p.m. to 8:00 p.m. practice time is, well, a bother. Conceding to convenience and environmental responsibility, I contacted Liz to discuss carpooling. The arrangements worked, and as it turns out, her daughter Anna has grown into a quiet but sweet, delightful in fact, preteen girl. For the brief time, I enjoyed her company.

Somewhere along the way, the family acquired a dog of their own, a large black creature who barks viciously when other dogs pass by her yard and who, so I hear, is a generally nasty being. Lest anyone infer that I have fully transcended my initial recoil and retreat, my fear and avoidance, I will confess that I get some satisfaction out of this twist of justice. My baser nature, though maybe a bit tamed and much of the time off-duty, can still be tempted to show its unholy face, reminding me that I have more ground to cover in working on my self.

The question of Zoey's guilt or innocence goes unanswered. But this episode, her supposed misbehavior and its repercussions, catalyzed for me an important, enduring, practice of self-care. I learned that I can shield myself from others' so-called "stuff," and now I do so. I remind myself of a Buddhist story. A revered monk was approached by one of his students. The disciple marveled at his teacher's ability to remain serene while, day after day, a stream of seekers brought to him their problems, frustrations, challenges, and complaints. "Teacher, how do you maintain your calm?", he asked. The monk answered in metaphor: "A guest comes to your door and offers you something. You do not like this gift, you see it is of little value to you, and so you do not take it. Who is left holding the gift?"

Perhaps anger, itself, is a teacher from which I can learn about my self, about the ways that I respond to situations, to others' emotions, about the interface between my past and present, the extent to which the past, though still making itself known, is also becoming healed. And perhaps anger is a gift, which I can simply choose to decline. Then, who holds the gift?

At the beginning of life, and again at its end, we squander our attentions on the mundane. As new parents, we focus on the most basic of physical tasks. Has the baby eaten enough? Slept? Wet her diaper? Is he warm enough, comfortable? Near death, regardless of the species of the one dying, we go through the same mental machinations. With Zoey, for example, despite the heavy emotional toll of her illness, despite the psychological and spiritual traumas which it has embedded in the present and near future, I have worried inordinately about... her nutrition.

Ambivalence or compunctions about food have never plagued Zoey, our local champion of speed-eating. About ingesting, one of her prime talents and joys, she has cultivated a sort of eclecticism, remaining admirably open-minded, inclusive we might say, about the range of possible objects that she could consider subject to this pleasurable activity. Tissues, for instance, Kleenex or any comparable brand. For years, Zoey maintained a long-standing penchant for tissues, the wadded-up, used kind, not fresh, neatly folded ones just pulled from the box. Used napkins possess a similar allure, as do other objects which we humans are done with – dirty underwear, muffin wrappers robbed of the muffin itself, empty sandwich baggies. Down they go, and it's best to stop speculation there. She also enjoys bugs, silverfish that occasionally stand out as they scuttle across the white linoleum of our kitchen floor, pill bugs rolled up tight on the concrete walkway leading to our front door, sometimes even an ant or two, implicated by proximity to the remains of a melted popsicle. We have often marveled at Zoey's goat-like ability to digest, or at least ingest and process, all manner of what are, by our definition, inedibles.

Around Halloween, candy wrappers have held a special appeal. Here just having encased chocolate seems sufficient to make the candy's outerwear tasty. While many dog owners worry about their dogs having near-fatal close encounters with chocolate, I have fretted about my pup's intake of the chocolate-associated, be it foil or plastic. Remarkably, her digestive tract seems unscathed. Any adverse reaction to chocolate? If so, she has concealed it well.

Zoey's ability to tolerate edible non-foods has diminished with her illness. Not long ago, she found, and consumed, a Band-Aid covering a cut on my daughter's knee. Her reasoning, I figured, was nobly protective, akin to "something's stuck to my puppy." She took it upon herself to right the situation by gently nibbling off the plastic strip, and then of course swallowing it. But the Band-Aid didn't stay down, nor did the supper which preceded it. This turn of events, posing a stark contrast to her usually robust digestion, I took as an ominous omen.

As of yesterday,s I'm faced with a sobering new, almost unthinkable, departure from reality as I'd know it: she has lost her will to eat. Though it was a lovely Friday morning, the weather inside my head was heavily overcast, clouds of immense worry casting long shadows over the internal and external worlds. When I returned from my morning laps in the pool, and roused my pup as usual, she barely lifted her muzzle, didn't perk her ears, didn't give her body the usual good shake, didn't reach her front paws ahead of her, arch her back, and stretch.

For years, Zoey has met the prospect of her morning walk enthusiastically or, in the case of cold or rainy weather, at least good-naturedly. More recently, she has been slow but generally willing, able to muster the energy to attempt the normal. This morning, she signaled no interest whatsoever. I picked her up, carried her outdoors, and watched powerlessly while she completed her morning tasks; her range of motion has become minimal, allowing her to cover only a tiny portion of our small yard. Back inside, she would ordinarily have pranced alongside me to the kitchen, or raced ahead, every cell in her body eager for breakfast. This morning, carried into the kitchen, she stood feebly on her shaky legs, her mouth closed. I coaxed; she refused. I coaxed again, and again, to no avail. Finally I gently deposited her in her doggie bed and covered her body, up to her ears, with soft towels.

Life must go on. At work that day, peering out at my computer screen through eyes bleary with a layer of tear, I accomplished a bare minimum.

Later that day, at home again and restored to ease by jeans and a sweatshirt, I sat beside Zoey with my young neighbor and friend, Michael. Separated in age by three decades, we were united by a shared sense of helplessness, of desperately wanting to make things different, but utterly lacking the ability to do so. We needed her to eat; her refusal of food signaled her inability to be herself as we've known her, and soon, her inability to exist at all. And so we tried everything. Eventually she humored us, which we interpreted as monumental victory: Zoey ate a hotdog. With relief and a mounting sense of hope, we tried her on chicken. Success, again! Our spirits soared.

This morning, Saturday, even mushy boiled chicken failed to motivate her. I soaked tidbits in organic free-range chicken broth and fed them to her by hand, plying her with one small dripping piece at a time, with only an intermittent acceptance punctuating the baseline of devastating rejections.

How do we know if another being wants to live? One of our most basic assumptions is that the living want to keep living. We confer on Life an intrinsic entitlement, a right to be, and we never question this right. Our debates, instead, address the opposite, the stopping of life, and our rules all concern preserving life, not letting it go.

Dogs, within the relative simplicity of their lives, give us a few clear indicators of their will to live. Eating is principal among them. Once an avid eater, Zoey now shows no pleasure in this life-sustaining activity. In hand-feeding her these morsels of soft meat, I'm pleading with her not so much to eat, but to *want to live*. Please, Zoey, hang on, *try*, don't give up. How can I convince her to make the effort, to go through the motions required for her, purely and simply, to stay with us?

Quality of life. So often our discussions or our tortured deliberations about the end of life focus on this concept, so global seeming and compelling, but also so vague. It's a bit like the notion of an ideal vacation – we know some of its parameters and, most importantly, how it would feel, but we're hard-pressed to pin down just what it would be, to narrow in on the specific one. Or sometimes it's more like a cloud, backlit by sunrays, shifting shape, changing color, riveting but ephemeral. What, exactly, makes for a life's quality? It is not just a matter of being able to do things, for one can perform the same physical acts, those once done vigorously and with gusto, but having lost all will to live, now do them feebly, with little energy and no heart for it. No, it's not the actions themselves, but the pleasure we are able to take in them; enjoyment – literally the infusing of joy into something, it seems, is integral to a life that has quality.

In our quest for quality of life, then, we might do well to consider the status of our pleasures. Big and small, what are they? Do we truly enjoy them? Are we connoisseurs, enjoying them as fully as we might? Are we grateful, appreciative, even reverent at times? Are we open to new possibilities, new experiences, exploration, expansion of our pleasures?

Zoey's lack of judgment about objects – in this case, the objects of potential eating – has, over the course of her lifetime, afforded her an abundance not only of information but of pleasure. Perhaps we humans limit ourselves unnecessarily. I am not advocating lowering our culinary standards, but opening our minds to a broader array of experiences, without prejudgment. For our discernment can easily cross a thin line into inhibition, preventing us from sampling life's full bounty. Zoey, lacking any concept of dirty, disgusting, unhygienic, unseemly, embarrassing, or juvenile, is free to experience whatever comes her way – be it a filthy rag, an empty tuna can, charred swordfish skin at the edge of my plate, or filet mignon. If she weren't open to the possibilities, she might never know many pleasures.

I, myself, am challenged by sushi. Not maki, the cute little rolls filled with tidbits of red pepper and avocado, salmon or tuna, and sticky rice, all wrapped in green-black seaweed, but the raw fish kind, chewy in texture and recently, perilously, alive. I understand, rationally, that uncooked seafood may be delicious, but my discriminating mind steps forward with caution and qualm, coloring my ability to enjoy it.

Oysters are another example. I have never allowed one, raw and slimy, to slither down my clean pink throat; the mere concept makes me squeamish. Only two years ago, I broke through the sound barrier, so to speak, and tasted my first oysters. Baked. The setting was a fine restaurant in Durham; in a romantic gesture, my date ordered an appetizer which featured an artfully small number of oysters, making their cameo appearance in a rich bath of butter, cream, garlic, and bread crumbs. The flavor was exquisite, the oysters, well, I tried. My mind linked them, even cooked, to their cousins, the ones who meet the same fate, but raw.

I have to wonder how many pleasures we filter through the lens of the mind, with its mostly unconscious screens of judgment. Jobs, relationships, choices of activities, habits and behaviors, any of these decisions – large and small, momentous and trivial – might lead to pleasure, and they also allow us further opportunities to restrict our options, to narrow the range of our possibilities. Can we keep an open, curious, even playful, mind while also discerning the worthwhile from the not-worthy-of-our-attention? Can we become more panoramic in our view, our scope of the enjoyable, without ceasing to appreciate refinement?

I return to Zoey's motivation in all things – to learn, to enjoy, to love, and to sustain herself. For our own pleasure and quality of life, we might just want to adopt a dog's yardstick.

24

I have a sentimental attachment to Zoey's first leash, a royal blue nylon weave, lightweight at only a half inch in width, scaled down from adult versions for our barely ten-pound puppy (in adulthood, a more hefty twenty-five). She had lived with us for a couple weeks before I broached the idea of an official Dog Walk, beyond just toddling at will, implying leash and collar and direction. I anticipated uneventfully slipping the collar over her head, clipping on the leash, and then, off we would go, walking (me) and trotting (Zoey) down the sidewalk. I would be abeam with pride and affection; Zoey, excited about exploring the great and unknown world lying, tantalizingly, beyond our yard.

Reality refused to comply. The first steps in this envisioned memorable occasion proceeded as expected: I did carry one adorable puppy, new baby-sized collar (adorned with paw prints) in place, out to our front walkway, set her down on tiny paws, and clipped on the color-coordinated leash. One of us was ready to go. The other, not so willing.

Zoey sat down on her haunches, telling me with emphatic body language a decided "no." This total rejection of the concept caught me utterly by surprise. By definition, dogs *love* to walk. Don't they? I stared in disbelief at my pup, resolutely settled on the gray concrete. To her puppy mind, I had to acknowledge, this tethered proposition didn't jibe with any reasonable desires for the out of doors – namely, to romp, explore, roam, sniff, chase, wander, or follow. Silly me.

Slowly overcoming my training in self-denial, acquired early in life and which I honed, over the years, into a reflex, I increasingly realize that, when meeting resistance, it's not only kind and caring, but wise and helpful, to do quite the opposite – not to withhold, nor to grit one's teeth and muscle through whatever the undesirable might be, but to sweeten the pot, to *treat*.

Out came the doggie cookies. Dog food companies shamelessly appeal to the nurturing instincts of their constituents, not dogs but dog-owners; they market dog treats shaped like the cookies that a mom would give her kids – piggy in blanket, strip of bacon, miniature sausage, and the ever popular fire hydrant. Being a discerning consumer, I had decided that Zoey would appreciate the classics – Milk Bones, the confections of my own childhood pups, Taffy and Tasha. There's something honest, wholesome even, about the simple bone shape and the plain cardboard color, most likely matched by cardboard taste. It could be that our youngest family member was in fact above consumer-directed gimmicks, or just that I conceded here, just a bit, to my frugal and denying tendency, ashamed as I am to air it. Fortunately, Milk Bones do offer some variety, for instance, teeny sizes for little mouths.

And so, with the aid of Milk Bones, coaxing, and praise, Zoey and I launched a nearly ten-year history of walking together, with initial progress measured in baby paw steps. First, we walked twenty yards to the neighborhood's communal mailbox, a piece of puppy-sized Milk Bone offered every few paces. Then to the street corner beyond the mailbox, a whopping one house past ours and maybe a hundred yards down the sidewalk, more cookie resulting. Before long, we could walk around the block, roughly a third of a mile that took anywhere from six to sixty minutes, depending on our motivation and who we bumped into along the way.

And then we opened a new chapter in our shared life, the several-years-long phase of the Bailey Walk. Bailey, fluffy white and purebred, a Bijon Frise who lived next door to us and was, in effect, a "shut in" due to his owners' work schedules, became Zoey's elder uncle. As a pup, Zoey could walk right under Bailey's belly when, that is, Bailey deigned to stand still for this antic. I know this to be historical fact, though I have no idea now how any dog, however young and miniscule, could fit underneath such a pint-sized lapdog.

Zoey was, indisputably, a quintessentially cute puppy. And tiny.

The Bailey Walk happened every Monday through Friday at lunchtime. It involved me, my two preschoolers, one of whom usually rode in the rickety collapsible stroller that served as daily conveyance, Zoey, and of course the ostensible reason for the adventure, Bailey. The five of us – four children of mixed species and one adult – looped once around the neighborhood, singing, telling stories, enjoying the outdoors and the dogs' companionable interactions. Bailey was still young and playful, and Zoey, the baby. As the years slide by and Sam, then Carolyn, left for school, I continued the ritual. With or without kids, I was glad to bring this ray of sunshine into my neighbor dog's life and to get outdoors mid-day, walking with my own pup. The Bailey Walk was, it seemed, an institution with a life of its own.

Inexplicably, years passed. The last time I saw Bailey (Donna, his owner, having moved to a new home a few years ago), he was an aging adult, stocky but healthy, solidly planted on the ground, unmistakably showing his fourteen years, fur thinning, moving a little stiffly.

Though an unwelcome intrusion at the outset, walks became one of Zoey's greatest joys in life, possibly surpassing even mealtime or tummy rubs. How many thousands of walks has she taken with me?

I remind myself, here, of a useful lesson: What evolved into one of Zoey's mainstay pleasures began in a frame of reluctance, with restraintv and requirement, a leash and a command, albeit a cajoling one.

At 45, I find myself reassessing many of the things I've done, semi-ritualistically, throughout my adult life. Family members, probably other onlookers too, have had their expressed and not-too-flattering opinions about my activities, which to them look like compulsions. I exercise at the crack of dawn every day; I go to bed early; I move around throughout the day, challenged to sit still; I declutter, almost pathologically. What has been driving me?

As a teenager, or more accurately a twelve-year old, I quite consciously yoked my sense of self and self-worth to numerous requirements. The logic went something like: if I *do* this, this, and this, then I will be OK. I never delved into the implicit question, and if I don't? In this way, as a preteen, I began a thirty-year campaign of self-improvement. I earned my keep, my place in the world, (or so I thought), by doing with unbending dedication any number of self-assigned or externally prescribed tasks. I simultaneously created, created *for myself* and out of a part of my self, a grim and unyielding task master. Needless to say, I made a stellar student.

Over the years, I've seen myself rise up from a succession of small deaths and surmount a series of impossibilities. Only gradually, through this process, have I realized that I deserve not harsh disciplining or strict requirements, but kindness. An encouraging word, a Milk Bone.

I see now that self-worth is not earned by doing, but by *being*, and as this concept sinks in, I demand less of myself. Without requirements compelling my activities, those activities qualitatively change their nature, they become choices… and I realize that I do, in truth, love my personal rituals. I love experiencing the early hours of the day, on weekdays when I get up to exercise, though I also now love to luxuriate under the covers for an extra hour on a weekend morning. I love to be outdoors in the predawn stillness, walking or running, spending time with my soul. I love to swim, to dance, to tune into my body in my yoga practice, to have silence and a clear peaceful space around me. I had thought that I needed a leash to keep me on track, to guide me in doing what I need to do, but, as it turns out, I don't. Choice, a form of freedom, makes light of requirement.

A couple weeks ago, I hung up Zoey's leash for the last time, morosely acknowledging that she had no further need of it. As her "normal" self, unleashed, she loved to dash away from a chasing Carolyn, to release her naughtiest aspect and tear off into a neighbor's backyard. She needed restraint, reining in, her leash. Now, simply, she doesn't. She doesn't need it because she can't any longer avail herself of the many temptingly delightful alternatives it precluded. This finality, and the absence of choice in it, feels both poignant and cruel. It confirms Zoey's helplessness in the face of her physical demise, and my heartbreaking inability to help preserve her, her body and her pleasures.

Zoey would love to have her leash in service, still allowing her the freedom of a long walk. I, on the other hand, by sheer virtue of my health and vitality, in dropping my self-imposed leash gain both my own freedom and my power to choose. There is no justice in this contrast, only reality.

Much as adversity brings out the best in people, death seems to unveil people's spirituality, a deep aspect of the self so often guarded, carefully, and protectively hidden. Natural disasters elicit a flood of generosity, compassion, energy, and concern – the essence of our spirit. And yes, too, in these times we open the valve that allows money to flow; one might argue that this bespeaks an effort of the spirit, the effort of giving, letting go of, and practicing generosity with something intimately associated with our security and self-worth. Great misfortune levels the playing field, stripping us of firmly set blinders – namely, our differences in personality and circumstance – and allowing us to see each other for our naked similarity. As fellow human beings. Similarly, death derobes us and exposes, beyond our common needs and feelings and experiences, our shared inner truths.

Last night, sitting cross-legged on my bedroom floor, my laptop open in front of me, Zoey sleeping nearby, I spoke by phone with Jason, with whom I've only recently begun working. Impressive though only in his late twenties, Jason has already launched a successful and rapidly growing non-profit, become chief technology officer of a new biomedical start-up, begun medical school (though currently he's on leave of absence so as to plunge headlong into other ventures), and completed coursework toward a PhD in computational biology. He appears not to need sleep; there may be slight impairment in his spatial relations, as he co-locates himself at Harvard and Duke, and often plans to be in both places simultaneously. He makes frequent appearances at high-level conventions and in meetings with high-and-mighty academicians and business-people. Jason is a whirlwind of energy and achievement.

My invitation to serve as freelance grant-writer for the start-up couldn't have come at a worse time. It arose unexpectedly in the form of an email, marked urgent with a red exclamation point, and bearing a single sentence. "Can you meet Dr. Paragon and Jason at 11:30 today?" Dr. Paragon is former President and CEO of a major local medical institution; the opportunity to assist his new company, even in some small way, could only be viewed as an honor. My answer, the only answer of course, was "yes."

Just the day before, I had suffered a direct hit by the proverbial bombshell, this time in the form of a phone call from Zoey's vet, delivering her diagnosis of cancer. I had, in no way, expected this news, which whipped through my psyche with the destructive force of an interior hurricane. Sleepless, I tossed and turned all night, my mind and emotions wracked. That morning, I had dressed my teary, weary self in black, which fortunately still defined sharp dressing in the professional lexicon, expecting a typical day in the office. And at 10:00 a.m., I received this email from Dr. Paragon's assistant, with marching orders – be there, 11:30. It couldn't be helped. I located the building, parked in the deck, exited the polished chrome elevator at the top floor, and appeared in the executive suite, a corner sweep spanned by floor-to-ceiling windows that afforded an expansive view, mostly green with buildings and dull stripes of street interspersed. Against this calm backdrop, I arrived at the appointed time, in a state of personal wreckage.

Briefly excusing my distraught appearance, I joined the short and efficient meeting which cut straight to the point. A half hour later, I walked out immersed in a strange mixture of grief and excitement, despair at an impending end and exhilaration at the prospect of a new, though uncertain, beginning. Based on the tenor of this meeting, and of several conference calls that followed, I formed a task-focused attitude toward the work ahead. These are, after all, medical *scientists*, and I would need to deliver. My heart's struggles would be my own business.

As the weeks passed, and as Zoey's physical and emotional condition took a nose-dive, I entered a dark phase of profound sorrow. The depth of my love was matched by the intensity of my pain, my unwillingness to face loss, my helpless anguish. Mercifully, one Saturday provided a reprieve. My pup came downstairs on her own, she ate (hand fed at first, then on her own), she drank, she perked up. My spirits rose, tentatively, cautiously, but with a fervent prayer. I sang to her. I began to hope, and determined myself to do everything possible to assist her in healing.

Meanwhile, as the grant deadline approaches, I have begun to communicate frequently with Jason. In these calls, we adhere strictly to business; I still, after all, stand on the judgment block at this organization, with my grant-writing contract serving as a trial balloon. Because I don't yet know how I will measure up, professionalism and efficiency hold sway over the temptation toward amiable conversation.

Desperate times, however, can change our perspective, can alter what we consider better judgment in situations immediately before us. As a young girl, I had a toy which was powerful in its simplicity: a child-sized burlap sack containing small slabs of transparent colored plastic, which I could hold up to my eyes and look through, seeing clearly but in different colors. The filters had a fascinating effect, changing the hue of everything in front of me, and by so doing, interestingly, also changing the look and feel of those things. Zoey's cancer has a similar filtering effect, shifting my perception of the world around me and, correspondingly, my response.

On this Saturday evening, as we wrapped up a phone call connecting Boston (Jason) to Chapel Hill (me), I made a previously unthinkable choice: I asked Jason if he remembered that my dog is sick. He had been there on Day

One, at our first meeting with Dr. Paragon which was, more momentously, the first day after I had received The Diagnosis, Zoey's. Now, I told him, she's not doing well. Jason's answer caught me off guard. "I'm really sorry. My dog died two weeks ago." Out of nowhere, a steamroller had suddenly appeared and driven onto the playing field. "She was 14. She'd had a good life. But I grew up with her, and she was always my dog when I was at home. My mom told me she just went out one day and didn't come back." And then, the most unexpected addition, stated as fact, "It's hard, but she's in doggie heaven and I know she's happy. I'll ask Rascal to be on the lookout for Zoey."

Now, I believe in the Other Side, and I do trust that Zoey will be comfortable, happy, and loved after she passes from this level of consciousness to the next. I do not, however, expect many people to share this view – especially not the scientists with whom I cross paths every day. Not to mention the mainstream Southerners surrounding me, with whom I never discuss my inner life; our interior worlds, I have believed, just don't intersect. But I realized last night, downstairs now and cradling a phone against one ear as I washed my supper dishes, that, in a couple sentences, Jason had dissolved huge concrete barriers of expectation, of difference, that I, myself, had erected. I had inferred from ways of working and interacting, from backgrounds and impressive dockets of expertise, from ways of dressing and talking and behaving, that others live in a different world from me, a world either non-spiritual or one defined in narrow religious terms that precluded our sharing common ground. I was wrong.

A little later, tucking clean sheets over my queen-sized featherbed, a weekly Saturday night ritual I perform to prepare a haven of rest, I thanked Rascal for being ready for Zoey, and in advance for welcoming her when the time arrives. And I will continue to send unspoken thanks to Jason for opening a crack in this window, for giving me a glimpse of shared belief. I had mistakenly formed an expectation of separateness based on an outer appearance, that of a cold, rational, task-oriented world, and had believed our inner realms too different to permit the solace of connection. I was wrong.

26

Zoey sometimes communicates with us in a distinctive way – using her nose. The tip of her nose, to be specific. In canine linguistics, I imagine, her strategy epitomizes discretion; she has chosen the poet's approach, the less-is-more philosophy rather than the more loquacious way of a canine dramatist or epic bard, who might be more inclined to exuberant slobbery licks. Zoey reserved her special nose-implemented communications for outdoor times which, to her, were public moments, observable by fellow members of the natural world (cats, squirrels, other dogs) or by human friends, neighbors, pedestrian and drive-by.

Walking along our typical figure-eight loop I call the Polo Walk, we traverse the bottom of our neighborhood, climb a hill, turn a corner onto a densely wooded street, green even in winter as only the Southeastern states can maintain. At the top of a short but steep hill, I listen for snippets of music wafting from the jazz pianist's house, then we continue down the backside of the hill, pass the houses of a Chihuahua, two grey mutts, an English sheepdog, and then regain elevation by trudging up a long curving swath of shady street.

Invariably, at some point along that daily pilgrimage, Zoey used to deliver a kiss. To me. Well-behaved on her leash, she never lagged far from my heels; this closeness allowed her to slip, unnoticed, near enough to give my calf a meaningful tap with her small, moist and shiny, black nose. This fleeting almost furtive touch is somehow more precious than any lavish, overt, declaration of love.

Not long ago, I pulled out a middle-sized cardboard box, flaps tucked under one another to close it. The box contained a loose collection of papers and miscellaneous items, a significant pen or two, a few seashells, ribbons for this and that – the physical remainder of my college memories. Stored at my parents' house in Massachusetts for many years, this carton found its way back to me, like a homing pigeon carrying messages about my earlier self, when my parents relocated to their dream home on the coast of southern Maine. I tucked it into our house's only storage closet, unopened.

My daughter, however, loves to pore over old photos and, one thing leading to another on a rainy day, I pulled out this now rather battered and worn-looking box. We excavated photos, papers, clippings, and cards, as well as the odd matchbook and memorable wrapper (remembrance of chocolates past). I read birthday cards from college roommates, friends' postcards that reached me overseas on my year of travel (how did they know which youth hostel I'd be at?!), cards from my parents, notes, in shaky handwriting, carefully penned by my grandmother. One card didn't strike any chords of memory. It was an anonymous valentine, red, floral, lovely, with a mushy Hallmark message on the inside, and signed "from one you take no notice of."

Except for a brief spell as a freshman dating a senior, I spent my college years as a bachelorette, and not by choice. My friends, roommates, and the inescapable squadrons of beautiful girls around campus all had boyfriends. I, instead, had crushes. No inquiries, and no interest in me, or so I thought. I cried my share of tears out of loneliness and frustration, and for what I interpreted as my own evident unlovableness. A reservoir of emotion welled up inside me, and I ached to pour this love out upon my heart's object. Nobody appeared; nothing developed. I graduated.

These days I understand, grudgingly, that God speaks in whispers. We miss the messages of spirit – of beauty, love, joy, wisdom – unless we maintain a deep quiet within ourselves. If we can dwell in that silent space and listen, with our eyes and ears and hearts, we hear God everywhere.

As a late teen and twenty-something in college, I wanted shouts, not whispers; I wanted love to come to me loud and clear. In my visions of a romantic relationship, the love was straightforward and spoken clearly – unequivocal, expressed, easy to see and feel. Alright, I confess, I clung to this ideal right up through my thirties, across my marriage and its demise, and even into my re-imaging of my life just after divorce.

What have I missed by requiring a twenty-decibel opera, rather than a barely perceptible murmur? Perhaps I have, unawares, left a trail of valentines behind me, delivered not necessarily (though hopefully) from men but from other souls whom I've helped or touched in some way – animals, children, plants, places, times.

The subtle dabs of Zoey's nose, so sweet, re-endear her to me each time, instantaneously and on the spot. They remind me of her love in a quietest possible way. They melt my heart. May I, too, find ways – pure and barely perceptible, like a feather's touch, lacking drama but felt nonetheless – to pass along the gift of my love to others.

Zoey's last day arrived, a harsh fact not at all mitigated by being known in advance; I had scheduled the day, and still it dawned in a wave of shock. I took the day off of work, recording it as a "discretionary day" on my timesheet because the idea of calling this a "vacation" offended me. Usually, on weekends or other non-working hours, I stay busy in the house, using extra moments to empty the dishwasher, fold laundry, vacuum, fight the perpetual battle to keep the kids' clutter at bay. This day, I had more urgent business. I had to sit with Zoey.

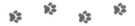

My life, probably like most, has marched on largely as an unending stream of tasks. Education, public school followed by college and graduate school, had its own set of requirements, then came those associated with work, parenting, home ownership, pets, plants, and all the assorted obligations and responsibilities that command that precious commodity, time. Added to these demands of context are those of self care, those things we must do to maintain and sustain ourselves – exercise, cooking and eating, brushing our teeth let alone going to the dentist. Tasks, requirements, activities, all form a history of continuous doing. Oddly, because we tend to define ourselves by our histories, we essentially become a collection of doings, many of them mundane or externally dictated.

As a graduate student in public health, I enrolled in several courses that required projects completed in teams. This irked me considerably. Having been a high-functioning student for the majority of my life, I had developed the art, or more accurately the science, of efficiency, organization, staying on top of assignments and completing schoolwork on a tight schedule, *my* schedule. Now the necessity of integrating my ideas with others in a team, working within the confines of *their* schedules, dividing the effort and preparing a combined end-product, all held me back. I was thwarted in my drive to *do*.

On one project, I sat in a circle, on a hardwood floor partially covered by a hodge-podge of second-hand oriental rugs, the ground of an apartment in Cambridge, with three female classmates. We were a team, convened to accomplish a project for Epidemiology. First, we sipped cups of herbal tea as we discussed health policy, griped about the homework assigned in Statistics, confided about relationships and goings-on in our lives. Did I enjoy this? No. My focus was firmly fixated on the project, a ticker tape running in my head: we have work to do, we need to stick with the task, the clock is ticking.

Given this inner pressure affecting me, and the way it must have come across to others – as aloofness? disconnection? unpleasantness? – it's a wonder to me now that I managed to maintain any friendships at all before I reached my forties. Alongside my compulsion to measure up, to accomplish my tasks and meet the requirements I heaped on myself, I must have had a knack for concealing my ugly, poorly handled urges to paddle hard as I struggled to keep my head above water, to survive, which meant, simply, to *do*. Or maybe I had forgiving friends.

My dog, by contrast, has had remarkably little drive to accomplish. Over the course of her life, she hasn't even mustered much interest in chewing, that staple of canine activity, unlike her peers who incessantly gnaw on sticks or rawhide treats. Do they feel an urge, a need or compulsion, in their distinctive dog way, to do? Zoey, by contrast, has perfected her ability to lounge, through years of practice, spending most of her daytime hours comfortably curled up on something soft. She excels at just simply *being*.

On Zoey's last day, March 13, 2006, my urge to do evaporated. Or rather, it dried up, left me, vanished into thin air. In its place, I only wanted to be with my dog, to merely exist alongside her, in her presence, quiet and together. This simple sharing of her final moments, an experience complete in itself, was more precious than anything I could have imagined. I thank her for this lesson.

28

I received the following email from my neighbor, Tanya, on the morning of March 14:

> Jane I am so sorry, really I do know how you feel. I noticed this Sunday there was lots of dogs barking around the neighborhood all afternoon. Last night Polo was acting very strange. He walked around the house somewhat confused. He barked a little but mostly just sat close to Colin or me (right on our toe) He didn't seem to want to have us leave him at all. He refused his dinner. When I took him out for his nighttime walk, he just walked aimlessly. Really it is amazing he seemed to know. His good friend died and he was depressed.

This gives me a good measure of solace. Polo, that gentle, male but unabashedly unmanly, adoring companion, has known Zoey for most of his life. I began walking the two dogs together when both were puppies, the two of them making a classic odd couple, one largish, shaggy, black/brown, loosely German shepherd-like and the other smallish, sleek, white with black markings, a terrier of sorts. Both mutts, good-natured through and through, and both clearly fond of one another. They walked shoulder to shoulder, sniffed the same bushes, bristled at the same cats just out of reach, strained toward the same squirrels, taunting from a safe distance. Zoey could have counted her weekdays in "Polo Walks," and Polo, likewise.

I arranged for Zoey to die at home. It was a Monday, an uncharacteristically balmy day for mid-March. With daffodils smiling at us from clumps planted randomly about our yard, Bradford pears in full snowy bloom, I carried Zoey outdoors one last time to show her the flowers and let her feel the warm caressing breezes on her face. She had lost weight over the past weeks; at just over twenty pounds and dropping, she's been no trouble to carry in and out, up and down stairs, to her doggie bed and her favorite cushions. Holding her close, I buried my face in her fur, kissed her forehead, murmured messages of love.

The weekend had broken my heart. From her diagnosis on Martin Luther King Day until this Saturday afternoon, though her tumor grew rapidly and progressively restricted her mobility, she did not seem to be in the daily sort of pain we associate with cancer — except when she tried to walk, the huge mass above her shoulder forcing a pronounced limp. Two weeks ago, with a heavy heart, I discontinued walking her. This confused Polo, my showing up at his door at 3:00 p.m., as always, but without Zoey. "Zoey's not feeling well," I told him, and on subsequent afternoons I would continue to keep him apprised of her status, "Zoey's still not feeling very good." Such were my feeble attempts to protect this dog-friend from sorrow and truth.

But on Saturday, late in the afternoon, my pup began to cry. I have told you this story, but in doing so, neglected to describe my futile attempts, day in and day out, to make sure she stayed comfortable, to reposition her, to soothe her, to calm her and, when bedtime came, to tuck her in and lull her to sleep. On this night, despite my lying next to her and rubbing her tummy, humming softly, she couldn't shut her eyes. The crying, intermittent and heart-wrenching, began. And continued. I've told the story of a late-night dash to the emergency veterinary service, with the help of a compassionate neighbor. We had gotten Zoey through the immediate crisis. For a few minutes. After many hours at veterinary emergency, and with two prescriptions for pain medications in hand, we returned home only to have Zoey's crying resume as soon as I set her down.

I must have dozed off. Arising from what I thought had been a sleepless night, I found that Zoey had been violently sick, the evidence splatted not once but twice. In tears, I cleaned up. To my delight, she drank a little milk at my coaxing. This, however, led to more tummy upset, and more clean-up. Her time, I knew, had come. I had rejected this concept for seven weeks, stubbornly trying remedy after remedy, grasping at hope, affirming (even flaunting to the kids) the slightest of positive signs, refusing the impending loss. But now, when I could see her suffering, the whole picture changed. Reality took on a very specific tone, a sort of sober inevitability. I could no longer deny or prolong the end; kindness and love required something different of me.

On Sunday, I called in to work, to request time off for the next day, Zoey's last on this earth, and my last day with her. I had planned to take her to the vet, a vague plan but firm. I lay with her much of the day, though in the late morning, I walked around some of the neighborhood streets to calm myself with time outdoors – my standard cure-all. A neighbor whom I know only slightly was outside working in his yard. Tall, handsome, fifty-something, he and his wife had moved into a newly renovated house overlooking a small lake, and he was tidying up the recently landscaped slope. "How are you doing?" he asked, most likely expecting the typical "fine" or possibly "great!," followed by the same question asked of him or some comment about the weather. "Awful," I replied. This was the truth. He raised a bushy gray eyebrow, and I explained. "It's my dog's last day, so I'm just home with her." Tears welled up.

My neighbor's eyes immediately registered that he understood. He leaned his rake against the fence, took off his work gloves, and sighed. "I used to have a greyhound," he began. And then I could place my memory of this newcomer to our neighborhood – nearly every morning, as I drove off to work, I had seen him and his lithe, elegant dog walking on the bike path. They crossed the field perpendicular to the street, and continued along the sidewalk, side by side, one elongated athletic body with another. I'd admired the refined dog, with matching human, often. "She died last year. She's buried back there," he motioned to his back yard. He had arranged for a vet come to the house, because "my dog *hated* going to the vet."

And so I wound up on the phone, in search of a vet who would be willing to make a house-call on short order. Soon I had an appointment set with Dr. Peterson, who would come to deliver a lethal injection after the kids got home from school. With this arrangement finalized, I returned to my pup's side, painfully conscious of the ticking clock. Zoey's hours, her minutes even, were numbered, and each moment with her became priceless. I had no desire other than to focus entirely on being with her, experiencing her presence, sitting with her soul. And when the vet arrived, I held her, and wept, the whole time.

Zoey's body now lies underground, in a side area of our yard, where we can look out at her from our table at breakfast and dinner. The image of her, so cute, curled up as if asleep, covered with a warm blanket that left only her face exposed, set to rest in a too-deep and inhospitable hole in the earth, haunts me. Maybe we'll plant some shade-loving perennials over this freshly dug ground. Forget-me-nots?

I have no idea what will help me heal this wound, this gaping raw hole in my heart. My kids will help. So will the necessity of preparing meals, doing laundry, going to work, carrying on. Polo will help. Today, at 3:00 p.m. promptly, I'll show up at his door by myself, and I'll tell him all about it. I think he'll understand my tears, if not my words.

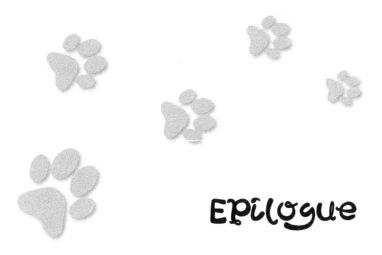

Epilogue

Entering through the garage, I provide the Protector of House and Home with numerous cues: the scrape of metal wheels on tracking as I manually raise the rickety garage door, the quiet hum of the hybrid engine as I roll my Prius into the garage, the open and shut of my Prius door. By the time I turn the doorknob and walk through the door, Maitri is on the job. Her paws stamp a little dance on the floor, as she restrains herself from jumping up on me; then, losing this internal battle, she leaps for my face, unable to resist the urge to lick. She is smiling, undeniably. Bouncing in circles around me, she exudes joy at my return.

There are similarities, yes, but many differences. For starters, both Zoey and Maitri are dogs. Like Zoey, Maitri loves food above all else, and defines it perhaps even more broadly than Zoey; she includes vegetable matter, which helps considerably in keeping down the volume of our compost. Apple cores, the funny little black piece at the end of a banana, green beans that are a bit too large – all are fair game. Like Zoey, Maitri loves to walk, to explore. Both are loving and affectionate. But where Zoey's fur was sleek, smooth, and sharply contrasting in black and white, Maitri abounds in fluff, and the palette of her coat covers many gradated shades of white, cream, tan, brown, and black. Zoey, an agile little athlete, leapt effortlessly into the car or onto my bed, a high-rise relative to her size. Maitri, though larger and presumably stronger, needs a helping hand. I remember her as a roly-poly puppy, falling off the curb at the side of the street; now almost four years old, she still sometimes mis-steps. Glancing back at me, she once walked into a tree.

There is, quite simply, no replacing a loved one – be it human, canine, or other. And so I can say without pretense or shame that I have not, at four years, "gotten over" the loss of Zoey. I remember her often, wistfully, longingly. I apologize to her for the years when I was distracted or overwhelmed, and failed to give her the attention she deserved. I remember her adorable face, her mannerisms, her funny ways; through these painfully transparent attempts, I suppose I am trying to keep her memories alive.

Over-sized mug of tea in hand, at the kitchen table, casually draped over a wooden chair, I look out the window to her burial spot, a shaded area under a small grove of red cedars to the side of the house. I did, in fact, plant a garden over her, carefully choosing from a high-end nursery a good number of shade-loving plants that I hoped would spread, fill in, and even bloom. But the blazing heat of southern summers, conspiring with my lack of time to tend the plot, to water and till and weed, has reined in my sentimental vision. A few of the original plants, the straggling vines and the hardier wildflowers, have taken matters into their own hands, loosely "naturalizing" the area, as it were. I sometimes feel that, in my failure to maintain her memorial, I've let Zoey down, and to assuage my conscience, I tell her again that I love her.

Maitri sleeps on my bed with me for some, to be disclosed, portion of every night. Usually she begins the evening in "her lair," meaning the low-ceilinged space underneath my bed, fitting her neatly up against the wall in the back corner of my bedroom. She is, to be sure, a fortunate dog to have her own lair (how many dogs can boast as much?), and she honors the privilege by decorating her lair with treasures. Empty (thoroughly cleaned by none other than herself) tuna cans, for example. Stolen items that would incriminate her if left in the open, such as the wrappers for chocolates she was never meant to have. Her beloved chew bones. A typical evening for Maitri begins in this cozy and well-appointed place, but as chill descends on the house, or perhaps as loneliness creeps in, she scrambles to the upper level to join me – her, on top of my down comforter, and me underneath. Her greeting licks are a veritable love fest, after our lengthy separation.

Zoey, I am sad to say, was never allowed on my bed. Had I known then what I know now, of the value of moments and the reality of ends, I would have welcomed her without the slightest concern for dirt borne on innocent paws, fur shed by wriggles and pats, or sleep disrupted.

If Zoey was the teacher, I have had Maitri to give me opportunities to practice what I learned. Her health issues as a puppy, for example, provided me two more chances to face death, its stark imminence, hopefully this time with greater wisdom and poise.

Most dog owners have heard of parvovirus, the dreaded disease that afflicts puppies; it wreaks a staggering 50% mortality for animals who receive treatment, 80% for pups who do not. Maitri made the brutality of these statistics dangerously intimate. We had scarcely had her for three days when the malady burst upon us from out of nowhere, shattering our delight with the new bundle of fluff, of cuteness incarnate, which we had just added to our family.

Maitri's arrival from a rural animal shelter in eastern North Carolina was carefully timed for the beginning of summer, allowing maximum time for Sam and Carolyn to acclimate her to our home while they were on school vacation. Carolyn, not having acquired the adolescent propensity to sleep until noon, was tasked with morning puppy-sitting. After a first weekend establishing routines for the new family member, most importantly the "puppybathroom" (one word, musically spoken) routine, I headed into the office on a sunny, warm, Monday morning.

Shortly after 9:00 a.m., Carolyn phoned. "Mom, Maitri's throwing up," she informed me, annoyance and only a slight concern in her voice. This event was not surprising, given that our babydog was a mere five weeks old; she had been one of ten puppies dropped at the shelter at one week old, along with their mother who decided to wean them at four weeks, likely due to exhaustion at nursing ten. This must have been a rough start, from the pups' standpoint, and we might well have expected some downstream consequences such as, perhaps, an immature gut. I coached Carolyn on cleaning up, and advised her to keep Maitri in the kitchen, barricaded by baby gates. Linoleum has its advantages.

Ten minutes later, the phone rang again. "Mom, she's still doing it." A note of urgency had crept into Carolyn's voice. The scene, apparently, was becoming alarming. "She can't go on forever, honeypie," I reassured her, "there's only so much that little tummy can hold." I imagined the tiny round belly, with its barest covering of fur, a physical expression of utter vulnerability. I coached Carolyn again on the logistics of managing the situation, pulling out clean but dispensable towels, laying down newspaper, having trashbags handy, washing hands frequently, staying calm.

And again, ten minutes later, another call interrupted my work. "Hang in there, I'm coming home," I told her, phone squeezed between shoulder and ear while hurriedly shutting down my computer and collecting loose papers. (In those days, I did not have a cell phone.)

In the thirty minutes it took me to get from my desk to home, little had changed. The kitchen was a mess, with blankets and towels covered with the pup's output, general mayhem, and Carolyn visibly distraught. "What are we going to do?? She won't stop," Carolyn wailed. The puppy, far from her usual playful and rambunctious, had turned listless, breaking her torpor only to vomit at intervals. I snapped into action mode: "We're going to the vet," I announced. And so we did, driving first to one vet, then another, then to the emergency veterinary hospital in Raleigh, twenty miles down the highway, and finally ending up many miles further away, at the offices of the vet who served the rescue agency through which we had found Maitri.

We found welcoming, though seriously concerned, hands. This vet's staff had, with the addition of Maitri, admitted half of the litter – five out of ten puppies – to their veterinary intensive care unit. Maitri was taken gently but firmly, hurriedly, from my arms. They whisked her away, through a closed door, into a back area that felt dangerously out of sight. For a full harrowing week, she teetered on the edge of death. We could do nothing but stand by, praying and hoping, calling often to check on her status. Of the five pups in the ICU with her, suffering through parvo together, two died.

Parvo works by destroying the lining of the dog's intestinal tract, so that bacteria can leak into the bloodstream and poison the animal, proteins and blood can seep into the intestines causing anemia, and the poor creature can't absorb nutrients. Dehydration, among various other complications, commonly leads to death. Puppies, with their immature digestive and immune systems, are especially vulnerable to this disorder. As soon as their systems can handle a vaccination, dogs are preventively inoculated; only very rarely does an adult contract the disease. Parvo works its destruction very fast, often killing the pup within a matter of days. But for those who make it through the first three or four days, in which the devastation has occurred and their system hit, full blast, there can come a turning point.

Maitri rounded that bend, after five interminable days in the ICU. Hearing the news of her ever so slight but definitive recovery, by phone on a weekday morning, quickly downing a bowl (OK, a mug) of oatmeal while standing in my closet choosing clothes for the office, I was washed through with a wave of relief. I quickly arranged to pick her up as soon as she was stabilized and, to the vet's opinion, in the safe zone.

On the appointed day, the head of the rescue agency, a kind man who had taken this whole disaster very much to heart, drove halfway to deliver my pup. Handing Maitri to me, gingerly, in a strip mall parking lot, he warned me of her fragile state, that she needed to be watched carefully. I reached out to reclaim her, instantly sobered by how little she weighed, by her fragility, her lack of substance. A young puppy, she had been little before parvo, but now she was tiny, reminiscent of a baby bird. Skinny and weak, she was alive – thank God!

Parvo had shone a light on the process of my inner attachments. I was startled to see how much I loved this pup already, after having "owned" her for just a handful of days. Through that long week, I had clung to a gritty insistence that she not die. I could not, would not, let her go, could not have another one torn away from me abruptly, too soon. I was determined, but powerless.

Back home again, Maitri's recovery was tenuous. In the first few days after her return, her gut could hold food, but she had lost the will to eat. We tried desperately to tempt her, to ply her with special puppy-relevant tidbits, but with no success. It was a tense, despairing, helpless time, all too reminiscent of Zoey's. And then, two days after her return, she tentatively took a small piece of boiled chicken, though colorless and flaccid, symbolizing life. She swallowed. Rejoicing! She was on the way.

I could tell, too, the story of this puppy's near death from encephalitis, just after she passed her first birthday, but truly, that would be just another in a stream of events, each begging inclusion. One lesson follows another in a continuous, sometimes flowing, sometimes intermittent, progression, an unfolding of life. Always in process, we never fully arrive, always have more to learn, always find ourselves presented with challenges that nudge, or force, us to do so.

Like Zoey, Maitri continues to teach me from the reservoirs of her own wisdom, and in the context of our shared experiences – one small furry creature who lives from her heart, who knows who she is, her likes and displeasures, her purpose; and one large creature who knows that she has much to learn.

CPSIA information can be obtained
at www.ICGtesting.com
Printed in the USA
BVHW082222140521
607267BV00004B/444